National Portrait Gallery
IN COLOUR

EDITED BY RICHARD ORMOND

WITH AN INTRODUCTION BY

JOHN HAYES

DIRECTOR OF THE NATIONAL PORTRAIT GALLERY

D1333644

STUDIO VISTA · LONDON

IN ASSOCIATION WITH THE

NATIONAL PORTRAIT GALLERY

CONTENTS

CONTRIBUTORS

Angela Cox
Robin Gibson
John Hayes
Richard Ormond
Mary Pettman
Malcolm Rogers
Richard Walker

Front cover: Ellen Terry, 1847-1928, Choosing,
by George Frederic Watts, 1864

Back cover: Isaac Oliver, c.1565-1617,
Self-portrait, c.1590

A Studio Vista book published by
Cassell Ltd,
35 Red Lion Square, London WC1R 4SG

and at Sydney, Auckland, Toronto, Johannesburg,
an affiliate of
Macmillan Publishing Co. Inc New York

Copyright © The Trustees of the National Portrait Gallery, London 1979
First published 1979

Designed by Logos Design

ISBN 0 289 70872 9
ISBN 0 289 70879 6

Printed in Great Britain by Sackville Press Billericay Ltd
Billericay, Essex, and bound by
Webb, Son & Co., Ltd, Ferndale, Glamorgan

INTRODUCTION

The National Portrait Gallery is a gallery of famous British faces. It was never intended to be a collection of the finest British portraits. Those who founded the Gallery in 1856 — notably the first Chairman, Lord Stanhope, a distinguished historian who was for thirty years President of the Society of Antiquaries — had not the slightest doubt about the historical role of the new institution. This is abundantly clear from their first Resolution, which continues to be strictly observed today: 'The rule which the Trustees desire to lay down to themselves in either making purchases or receiving presents, is to look to the celebrity of the person represented rather than to the merit of the artist'. This was not a new concept. Precisely the same formula had been adopted by the Governors of the British Institution when, in 1820, they held an exhibition of 183 portraits of 'Distinguished Persons in the History and Literature of the United Kingdom'. Stanhope, who may or may not have seen the exhibition itself — he was fifteen at the time — would certainly have possessed the catalogue and had this precedent in mind.

Nor was the idea of a 'gallery' of portraits at all new, though its manifestations had taken various forms throughout history. Commemoration of the notables of the day through portraits, a recognition of individual achievement and family power characteristic of the Renaissance and the age of Humanism, became common practice in fifteenth-century Florence. As early as the 1420s Masaccio included a mass of portraits of distinguished Florentines, some of them strictly commemorative, as the sitters were no longer living, in his frescoes for the church of the Carmine. Later, the Medici, like other ruling classes, came to regard portraiture as part of the trappings of the state. In Renaissance France, the fashion was for a cabinet of portraits of the great; Francis I and his court were commemorated in a series of fine chalk drawings by Jean Clouet, of which sets were repeated for the French nobility. Eventually, in 1833, Louis Philippe founded 'un musée de l'histoire de France' at Versailles. This still exists. In England, Lord Lumley, in Elizabethan times, was the first to bring together an important collection of historical portraits not confined to his own family or circle — or indeed to his own countrymen, or a particular epoch. Many a long gallery

The National Portrait Gallery (designed by Ewan Christian, 1896) from the north-east.

faintly echoed this ideal, and its owner looked up at Roman emperors or medieval kings as well as upon his ancestors, relatives and powerful connections. Lord Clarendon, first minister to Charles II, had rather different, and perhaps more personal, motives for forming the celebrated collection of portraits which hung in his mansion in Piccadilly. One was to assemble portraits of the participants in the Civil War and Interregnum, to animate his *Great History of the Rebellion*, and he was the first to use identical frames (the so-called Clarendon frames) to emphasize the effect of a gallery of portraits. From this it was only a step to the idea of publishing volumes of biographies with accompanying engravings. The most important of these was Houbraken's *Illustrious Heads*, which came out in parts from 1732 onwards. Their many counterparts in the early nineteenth century — Lodge's four folio volumes of 1821-34, or Knight's eight-volume set, handier in format, published in 1833-7 under the auspices of the Society for the Diffusion of Useful Knowledge — reflected Carlyle's interpretation of history as the biography of great men, a viewpoint which was fundamental to the idea of the National Portrait Gallery.

Both biographies and portraits fulfilled a moral as well as an educational purpose. As early as 1661 Evelyn declared that the busts of great authors which have traditionally adorned libraries — the Wren Library at Trinity College, Cambridge, is a fine example — were intended to spur

The National Portrait Gallery at Bethnal Green Museum, 1885. Portraits of the Restoration period.

The main gallery on the first floor of the National Portrait Gallery, at the time of the opening of the building in April 1896. Drawing by H.W. Brewer.

the reader on to equal feats. Such busts also served a legitimate national pride; Poets' Corner, in Westminster Abbey, is a phenomenon of the 1720s. Only a few years earlier Jonathan Richardson, in his essay on 'The Theory of Painting', wrote of portraits 'that men are excited to imitate the good actions, and persuaded to shun the vices of those whose examples are thus set before them'. How exactly this anticipates Lord Palmerston's advocacy of a National Portrait Gallery, in the Parliamentary debates of 1856! 'There cannot, I feel convinced', the Prime Minister declared, 'be a greater incentive to mental exertion, to noble actions, to good conduct on the part of the living, than for them to see before them the features of those who have done things which are worthy of our admiration, and whose example we are more induced to imitate when they are brought before us in the visible and tangible shape of portraits'.

Why, one is impelled to ask, was the Gallery not founded long before 1856, perhaps in the decades following Waterloo, and why was it founded just then — when the country was recovering from the aftermath of an inglorious war, the Crimea, and, with £42,000,000 added to the national debt, stringent economy was being practised in public expenditure? Part of the answer must lie in the pertinacity of Lord Stanhope, who, with the example . of Louis Philippe's portrait gallery at Versailles very much in his mind, proposed the idea in Parliament first in 1845 and again in 1852, and also with Prince Albert's concern about the accommodation of the national art collections in general. But the real answer is that it prospered on a flood tide. In spite of the impact of Darwin on Christian belief and of foreign competition and technological education on British industrial supremacy, the second half of the nineteenth century was an age of optimism and indeed complacency. The Victorians were ready for heroes. The Great Exhibition of 1851 demonstrated to millions the power of the machine and the growing conquest of the physical world. Herbert Spencer, who propounded a theory of progress and the perfectibility of man based on the law of evolution, was the most influential philosopher of his day. Thomas Arnold, in his inaugural lecture as Regius Professor of Modern History at Oxford (1841), went so far as to say that 'all is explored' and that contemporary history 'appears to bear marks of the fullness of time, as if there would be no future history beyond it'. The whole vast enterprise of the *Cambridge Modern History* (perhaps Lord Acton's most memorable achievement), of which the prospectus appeared in 1898, was inspired by something of the same belief. Small wonder that the Victorians, motivated by the doctrine of *laissez-faire*, were not only hard-working but also self-confident and self-righteous. Seeley's history of the British Empire, significantly entitled *The Expansion of England*, which appeared in 1883, sold eighty thousand copies in two years; and Joseph Chamberlain arrogantly called the British 'the greatest governing race the world has ever seen'. Throughout the whole of this period G.F. Watts was engaged on his portraits of eminent contemporaries, which he intended should be hung together as a 'Hall of Fame'; forty-two were later presented or bequeathed to the National Portrait Gallery. These were the perfect embodiment of one of the principal aims of the new Gallery: to encourage portraitists 'to soar above the mere attempt at producing a likeness, and to give that higher tone which was essential to maintain the true dignity of portrait painting as an 'art'.

The administration of the National Portrait Gallery was vested in a distinguished Board of

The gallery covering the years of the Civil War, as it is now.

Trustees. Disraeli and Macaulay were on the original Board; the first vacancy was filled by Carlyle and the second by Gladstone. The Trustees' primary concern has always been with acquisitions, with the selection of those to be represented in the Gallery; Stanhope's view was that entry to the 'national pantheon' should be severely restricted, and that not a single portrait should be admitted which would cause a person of good education to ask himself 'Who is he?' It was recognized from the outset that there were inherent difficulties — lack of historical perspective and the possibility of prejudice — in the selection of living sitters; not until recently has the rule debarring the admission of a living person (save the sovereign and his or her consort) been modified, and then only with careful safeguards.

The Gallery's original premises were quite modest: the first and second floors of No. 29 Great George Street, Westminster, close to the Houses of Parliament. The rooms were not opened to the public until January 1859, by which time seventy portraits had been acquired, and even then admission was restricted to Wednesdays and Saturdays. Later the Gallery moved to larger quarters, first at South Kensington, then at Bethnal Green. Both proved unsatisfactory: the premises next to the India Museum were a fire risk, and at Bethnal Green the pictures cracked. Conditions can hardly be said to have lived up to the Gallery's ideals. The present building was the gift of William Henry Alexander, a rich property owner and a benefactor of the arts, who stipulated Ewan Christian, a little-known church builder, as architect, and the Gallery opened here in St Martin's Place in April 1896. An extension built in the early 1930s from funds provided by Sir Joseph (later Lord) Duveen provided room for expansion. The space at our disposal has, however, become hopelessly inadequate for our present needs and service to the public, and a new building was approved in principle by the Government in 1971.

The arrangement of the collection has always been chronological. In the nineteenth century the portraits were displayed like specimens in showcases, packed along the walls, one above another, conforming closely to the Victorian concept of the specialist museum — what T.H. Huxley called a 'consultative library of objects'. A process of thinning, so that the pictures could be appreciated better, was begun shortly before the First World War, and this policy was continued until comparatively recently. The present concept of the permanent display is radically different in intention: the Gallery is now arranged as an illustration of themes in British history, with maps, objects and other associative material to complement the portraits and provide some relief from the rows of faces.

Under the first Director, Sir George Scharf, who was in charge of the Gallery from 1857 until 1895, some one thousand portraits were acquired, mostly by donation. Scharf's series of notebooks recording every work submitted to the Trustees with meticulous drawings and notes is a prized memorial to the thoroughness and scholarship which he made a hallmark of the Gallery's work. The grant-in-aid was a mere £750 and remained so until the early 1950s, any increase or special grant continually being vetoed by Victorian Chancellors of the Exchequer on the grounds that the Trustees professed themselves unconcerned with artistic merit — and hence its corollary, expensive pictures. Now there are over eight thousand works in the collection, as well as an immense archive, and the range has widened. Caricatures, disregarded in the early days of the Gallery's history since they were not ennobling, are now rightly recognized as one of the most searching forms of portraiture, precisely because partial and subjective. Photographs, totally neglected by the Gallery until the present century, in spite of the Victorian craze for the new medium and the fact that it had been taken up with enthusiasm by Queen Victoria herself, have been collected systematically since 1968, the year of the Cecil Beaton exhibition. More significantly, as history has long since ceased to be regarded as the story of men of destiny but rather as a flux which at any given moment individuals can hope only partially to understand or to control, a greater number of distinguished men and women, from many more walks of life than were previously accepted as worthy of recognition, have been admitted to the collections. The pages which follow reflect the living tissue of five centuries of British history.

THE MIDDLE AGES

The Middle Ages are remote in time, and divided from us by a deep cultural and philosophical gulf. It is difficult to grasp the temper of medieval thought, with its theologically orientated systems, or to understand the structure of its society and institutions. The stirring events of the time, the extraordinary adventure of the Crusades for example, still have a strong hold on our imagination, but we know little about the way in which medieval people thought and felt.

Visual records are fragmentary and difficult to interpret, and of portraits in the conventional sense there are hardly any. It is not possible at this period to chart the course of British history through the likenesses of its great men, as the rest of this book attempts to do. The Gallery possesses only a handful of medieval portraits, and they are mostly regal. The idea of recording the likeness of a particular individual was alien to the medieval mind, which regarded man as a lower form of creation in a universe dominated by the idea of God.

Representations of early English kings figure on objects associated with the royal administration, like coins, seals, and charters, but as token symbols only. There is no attempt to give the human form any individuality. What was important was the office of kingship and its continuity. Without the help of inscribed names, it would be difficult to tell one king from another on the coinage. Features are no more than a series of blobs for eyes, nose and mouth, and the design follows a limited range of patterns. It is significant that the coinage of William the Conqueror differs little from that of his Saxon predecessors, and that no attempt is made to distinguish his coinage from that of his son, William II, by the addition of a numeral. Seals are a more elaborate expression of the powers vested in the monarchy, but they are no more illuminating as portraits. A change of seal invariably accompanies a change of ruler. Only in this way can the new king demonstrate his succession and his legal right to command.

Images of kings exist in manuscript illuminations and stained-glass windows, but the most significant medium as far as portraiture is concerned is sculpture. From the time of Henry II in the late twelfth century there is an almost unbroken sequence of tomb effigies, in stone, marble, alabaster and bronze. The earliest effigies are idealized and hieratic, but from the time of Edward III sculptors do seem to have made efforts to record the features of the dead monarch, often making use of death-masks. In the case of Richard II the evidence of his appearance from his effigy is corroborated by two rare and important paintings, the full-length picture at Westminster Abbey and the famous Wilton Diptych in the National Gallery. Panel portraits of later medieval kings, like Henry V and Edward IV, are the work of Tudor workshops, and it is difficult to assess their authenticity as likenesses. Not until the sixteenth century does there exist a realistic tradition of portraiture.

1   RICHARD II 1367-99. Reigned 1377-99
By J. Randall, copy of the painting in Westminster Abbey

Richard succeeded his grandfather, Edward III, aged ten. During his minority, the nobility took advantage of his weakness to diminish royal power. Later Richard vigorously and savagely retaliated. The nobility felt threatened further by his advanced views on the authority of kingship and resented his sophisticated court. His cousin, Henry Bolingbroke, rallied sufficient support among the alienated nobles to depose him, and Richard died mysteriously at Pontefract Castle. This portrait is a copy of the earliest contemporary painting of an English king.

These tiny silver coins are not
strictly portraits. The images
are stylized and symbolic, and
there was no attempt at a
likeness.

Top
2   KING ALFRED
Reigned 849-901
Silver penny, c.887

Second row
3   EDWARD 'THE
CONFESSOR' Reigned 1043-66
Silver penny, 1065

4   EDWARD 'THE
CONFESSOR' Reigned 1043-66
Silver penny, 1065

Right
5   WILLIAM I 1027-87
Reigned 1066-87
Silver penny, 1068-71

Bottom right
6   WILLIAM I 1027-87
Reigned 1066-87
Silver penny, 1068

7   HENRY III 1207-72. Reigned 1216-72

Electrotype of the effigy by William Torel in Westminster
Abbey.

The son of King John, Henry III's long reign is notable for
the first Parliament, which met in 1264. Henry's dependence
on his French wife's relations, and the expense of fruitless
wars, led to a barons' revolt. Their leader, Simon de
Montfort, sought to strengthen the opposition against Henry
by summoning knights and burgesses to join the barons'
assembly. Henry was pious, scholarly and a discerning
patron of the arts. Westminster Abbey, for which this tomb
effigy was commissioned by Edward I in 1291, is the finest
tribute to his patronage. This is an electrotype made from
the bronze effigy.

RICARDVS · III · ANG · REX ·

Below

9 EDWARD IV 1442-83. Reigned 1461-70 and 1471-83
By an unknown artist

Edward owed his throne to the support of his powerful cousin, the Earl of Warwick. However, Warwick switched allegiance to the Lancastrian party after Edward's marriage to Elizabeth Woodville. Warwick and the Lancastrians were defeated in 1471 and Edward restored royal authority. He was self-indulgent and enjoyed a luxurious and artistic court. This image is based on a possibly contemporary portrait from life.

8 RICHARD III 1452-85. Reigned 1483-85
By an unknown artist

Richard's reputation was deliberately blackened by his Tudor successors. During the reign of his brother, Edward IV, he proved an able and respected administrator. When Edward died, Richard became Protector of his young nephew, Edward V. However, he distrusted the rapacious Woodvilles, relatives of Edward's wife, Elizabeth, and felt his own future at risk unless he seized power himself. Within three months he was king. Richard's support was seriously weakened by the unexplained disappearance of Edward's sons, the 'Princes in the Tower', and the death of his own son. Richard was defeated and killed at Bosworth by the Lancastrian faction led by Henry Tudor. There is no contemporary evidence for his disfigurement. Richard's portrait is derived from a contemporary painting.

10 HENRY V 1387-1422. Reigned 1413-22
By an unknown artist

A brilliant military and political strategist, Henry diverted the nobility from dissension at home to conquest abroad. He renewed the English claim to the throne of France and sought to recover the territory lost by King John. Henry's success was spectacular. He recaptured Normandy, married the French king's daughter and was recognized as his heir. Tragically, Henry died suddenly at thirty-two. This portrait may derive from a genuine likeness.

THE EARLY TUDORS

The early Tudor period is dominated by the figure of Henry VIII. Peace and stability had been established by his much shrewder father, Henry VII, after more than a century of civil war, and he bequeathed to his son a secure dynasty and a full treasury. Henry VIII threw caution to the winds, embarked on hazardous adventures overseas, and disported himself as a grandiose Renaissance prince, with a passion for building and a genuine love of scholarship and the arts. His matrimonial problems led to the famous divorce from Catherine of Aragon, the breach with Rome and the reorganization and despoiling of the Church. A legislative programme was put through Parliament that radically altered the structure of the state and society. Henry remained conservative by nature but events forced on him momentous political and religious changes. His reign saw the end of medieval institutions and the growth of the modern state.

The new men who surrounded Henry were energetic, ambitious and often unscrupulous. The price of failure was usually execution. Thomas Wolsey, whose heart was set on the papacy, dominated the political scene for the first twenty years of the reign, a man of great abilities but overweening vanity. He was succeeded by the cunning and ruthless Thomas Cromwell, who reorganized the royal administration, and by the wily Thomas Cranmer, Archbishop of Canterbury. The saintly Thomas More was one of the victims of the Henrician revolution, who refused to bend his conscience to accommodate his master. Anyone who thwarted Henry was liable to death or disgrace, and wives were no exception. Anne Boleyn and Catherine Howard were executed for alleged infidelity, Anne of Cleves was quickly pensioned off, Jane Seymour died naturally, and only his last queen, Catherine Parr, outlived him.

Though an overbearing tyrant to his subjects, Henry was also one of the most discerning patrons of the arts to sit on the English throne. Foreign artists and craftsmen flocked to his court to help build the palaces for which he is famous, Whitehall, Hampton Court and Nonsuch. And Henry himself and his court were immortalized in the portraits of Hans Holbein, one of the great masters of the northern Renaissance. His powerfully naturalistic style must have had tremendous impact in a country which was an artistic backwater. Within a few years England absorbed the latest European styles.

The reigns of Henry's successors saw the intensification of religious and political conflicts. Neither Edward VI nor Mary I enjoyed anything like the authority of their father, and the strong Reformation government of the former led to the equally extreme Roman Catholic reaction under Mary.

11   HENRY VII (1457-1509) AND HENRY VIII (1491-1547)
By Hans Holbein, 1536-7

Holbein's most important commission from Henry VIII was a massive wall painting for the Privy Chamber in Whitehall Palace. This life-scale drawing is part of the cartoon (working design) perforated with tiny holes to transfer the outlines to the wall. The complete painting included Elizabeth of York and Jane Seymour, Henry VIII's third wife and mother of his son. The huge bejewelled bulk of Henry VIII contrasts with the slim, pensive figure of his father. The painting was destroyed in a fire in 1698.

12 HENRY VII 1457-1509. Reigned 1485-1509
By Michiel Sittow, 1505

Henry Tudor defeated Richard III at the Battle of Bosworth in
1485 and claimed the throne as heir to the House of Lancaster.
In 1486 he married Elizabeth of York to unite the royal factions
and put an end to civil war. Henry's firm, shrewd and efficient
government established the Tudor dynasty and enabled his son
to succeed unopposed. The country prospered in a climate of
peace and the careful fostering of overseas trade. This portrait,
the first fully-documented one of an English king, was commissioned for Margaret of Austria in 1505. Henry considered
marrying Margaret, daughter of Emperor Maximilian, after
Elizabeth's death. Painted from life in the meticulous tradition
of the northern Renaissance, the face has a vivid individuality
hitherto unknown in English portraiture. Henry holds the red
rose of Lancaster and wears the Burgundian Order of the
Golden Fleece. The marriage did not take place.

13 ELIZABETH OF YORK 1465-1503
By an unknown artist

Daughter of Edward IV and Elizabeth Woodville, Elizabeth
became Edward's heiress after the death of her two young
brothers in the Tower. It was expedient for Henry VII to marry
her, as the Yorkist claimant to the throne. She was beautiful,
gentle and pious, and Henry became devoted to her. Of their
seven children, four survived childhood. The sudden death at
fifteen of her elder son, Arthur, was a terrible blow. She died a
year later in childbirth, leaving her husband grief-stricken. This
portrait is a version of the only painted image of Elizabeth. She
holds the white rose of York.

Opposite top
14 HENRY VIII 1491-1547. Reigned 1509-47
By an unknown artist, 1520s

Intelligent, cultivated and athletic, Henry VIII appeared the
perfection of kingship when he acceded, aged seventeen. The
lack of a son to ensure the succession led Henry to divorce
Catherine of Aragon, and to break England's allegiance to the
Church of Rome. Although he made himself Head of the
English Church and authorized the dissolution of the
monasteries, he kept the Reformation in check. Henry married
six times and was survived by his last wife, Catherine Parr, and
by his daughters Mary and Elizabeth, and his only son Edward.
In later life he became tyrannical, ruthless and obese. This
portrait dates from the 1520s when Henry had grown a beard
in emulation of the king of France: 'he is tall of stature, very
well formed, and of very handsome presence.'

15 CATHERINE OF ARAGON
1485-1536
By an unknown artist

The failure of Catherine, Henry VIII's first wife, to bear a son made Henry doubt the legality of their marriage. Poignantly, she holds a sprig of corn, traditional symbol of fertility; only her daughter, Mary, survived childhood.

16 ANNE BOLEYN 1507-36
By an unknown artist

Henry married Anne secretly in 1533, having failed to secure the Pope's sanction to his divorce from Catherine. Again, he was bitterly disappointed that she had no son. Anne made enemies at court, and in 1536 was executed on false charges of adultery. This portrait gives little evidence of her bewitching charm, though her dark colouring fits contemporary descriptions. This image, authenticated by the B-shaped pendant, is the standard portrait of Anne, of which several examples survive.

17 CATHERINE PARR 1512-48
Attributed to William Scrots, c.1545

Catherine Parr, Henry's sixth wife, whom he married in 1543, was popular with his ministers and his children alike. After Henry's death, she married Thomas Seymour, uncle to Edward VI, but her happiness was short-lived, for she died in childbirth a year later. This portrait is the only authentic likeness of Catherine.

18 SIR THOMAS MORE (1477-1535), HIS FAMILY AND DESCENDANTS
By Rowland Lockey, partly after Hans Holbein, 1593

In 1526, the great Dutch scholar, Erasmus, recommended the painter Hans Holbein to his friend Thomas More. For a year Holbein lived with the Mores at their house in Chelsea. In 1527, he completed a large informal group portrait of Sir Thomas and his family — a household renowned for its learning and hospitality. This picture perished by fire in 1752, but in the 1590s, Thomas More II, grandson of Sir Thomas, had commissioned at least three versions of it, by Lockey, one being an exact copy. Another, this picture, is a pictorial genealogy demonstrating the unswerving loyalty of later generations to the Roman Catholic faith. The family of Thomas More II, who suffered as recusants, are introduced on the right, replacing three figures that appeared in Holbein's picture. This accounts for the curious composition and combination of artistic styles.

19 SIR THOMAS MORE 1477-1535
After Hans Holbein, 1527

Scholar, statesman and finally martyr, Sir Thomas More is one of the best-known and admired figures of the sixteenth century. His book *Utopia*, a personal vision of an ideal state founded upon Reason and Philosophy, was published in 1516. Two years later he began his service to Henry VIII that culminated in 1529 in the highest office — Lord Chancellor. More resigned in 1532 to avoid the issue of Catherine's divorce and Henry's break with the Roman Church, which was anathema to him. Henry's relentless determination to bend More to his will brought about his conviction and execution for treason. This is the earliest and best copy after Holbein's masterpiece of 1527. More's gold chain signifies royal service, but beneath the splendid velvet and fur he habitually wore a hair shirt.

Above left
20 ARCHBISHOP WILLIAM WARHAM 1450?-1532
After Hans Holbein, 1527

For ten years, Warham combined the highest secular and clerical offices: Archbishop of Canterbury, 1503-32, and Lord Chancellor, 1504-15. He was involved in the initial proceedings for Henry's divorce. Though reluctant to comply with Henry's coercive tactics, he was too old and temperamentally unsuited to withstand the attack on the clergy. This portrait of the aged scholar and diplomat is a copy of Holbein's original painting.

Above
21 ARCHBISHOP THOMAS CRANMER 1489-1556
By Gerlach Flicke, 1546

Cranmer became Archbishop of Canterbury in 1533, supported Henry's divorce and subsequent marriage to Anne Boleyn, and accepted the Royal Supremacy. During the reign of Edward VI, he was a member of the Regency Council, and as Edward was dying he acquiesced in the plot to exclude Princess Mary from the succession. For this, and for his heresies, he was stripped of his authority when Mary became queen, and later burned at the stake. *The Book of Common Prayer*, published in 1549, is a testimony to his scholarship. Cranmer's portrait echoes the pose of Holbein's Warham.

22 CARDINAL THOMAS WOLSEY 1475?-1530
By an unknown artist

For nearly twenty years, Wolsey was the most influential man in England after the king: Archbishop of York from 1514, Lord Chancellor and Cardinal from 1515, and Papal Legate in 1518. His pride, ostentatious wealth and abuse of clerical power made him many enemies. His failure to secure the Pope's cooperation in the matter of Henry's divorce brought about his dismissal in 1529. This is the only known painted image of Wolsey.

23 SIR THOMAS WYATT 1503?-42
After Hans Holbein

Courtier and one-time lover of Anne Boleyn, Sir Thomas Wyatt is best remembered as the poet who (with the Earl of Surrey) introduced the Italian sonnet into England. As an ally of Thomas Cromwell, he was briefly imprisoned in the Tower in 1541. His portrait is probably based on a woodcut designed by Holbein.

Below
24 JOHN BOURCHIER, 2nd BARON BERNERS 1467-1533
By an unknown Flemish artist, 1520-6

Lord Berners was a statesman and scholar in the service of Henry VIII, whom he attended at the Field of the Cloth of Gold in 1520. He translated Froissart's *Chronicles* while he was deputy of Calais (1520-33), where this portrait was almost certainly painted. The meticulous style of painting and the placing of the left hand, which is similar to the portrait of Henry VII, support the attribution to a Flemish artist.

25 THOMAS CROMWELL, EARL OF ESSEX 1485?-1540
After Hans Holbein, 1534

Thomas Cromwell became prominent in Wolsey's service. However, Wolsey's dismissal in 1529 and More's refusal to be involved with Henry's divorce enabled Cromwell to influence the king decisively and effectively in the 1530s, and to consolidate royal power with the cooperation of Parliament. He masterminded the dissolution of the monasteries and arranged Henry's fourth marriage, to Anne of Cleves. His downfall came a year later, and he was executed for treason. Cromwell's cool determination pervades even the copy of Holbein's portrait.

26 LADY JANE GREY 1537-54
Attributed to Master John, c.1545

Granddaughter of Henry VIII's sister, Mary, Lady Jane Grey was the unwilling and innocent victim of court politics. If the claims of Henry's daughters, Princesses Mary and Elizabeth, were declared void, Lady Jane Grey would be the nearest Protestant heir to the throne after Edward VI. In 1553 she was married to Guildford Dudley, son of the Duke of Northumberland. Fearing the loss of his personal power if Catholic Princess Mary succeeded the dying King Edward, Northumberland persuaded him to will the throne to Jane. Queen Jane was proclaimed, and reigned for nine days. Mary had swiftly rallied support for her rightful claim, and Northumberland and his family were captured and imprisoned. Lady Jane and Guildford would doubtless have lived on, but Wyatt's rebellion a year later, although they played no part in it, demonstrated that they could be a focus for discontent. They were both executed. In this portrait Jane is aged about twelve. Her magnificent dress is of cloth of silver and lined with ermine, revealing an underskirt of crimson embroidered with gold braid and pearls.

27 EDWARD VI (1537-53) AND THE POPE
By an unknown artist, c.1548

Although Henry VIII had endeavoured to steer a middle course in
religion between Catholicism and Protestantism, he appointed a
Council of Regency for Edward dominated by ardent Reformers. The
Council lost no time in attacking the Roman Church. In February
1548, a proclamation authorized the wholesale destruction of all holy
images. This picture is an anti-papal allegory. Henry VIII, on the left,
points to Edward enthroned in the centre. Standing beside him is the
Duke of Somerset and round the table are seated the Duke of
Northumberland, Archbishop Cranmer, the Duke of Bedford and
four unidentified gentlemen. The Pope and his monks are being
vanquished by the true word of the Lord, while the buildings and
images of the Roman Church (inset top right) are being destroyed.

28 EDWARD VI 1537-53. Reigned 1547-53
Studio of William Scrots, c.1546

Born at Hampton Court, Edward was the anxiously-awaited son of
Henry VIII and Jane Seymour. Precocious, self-willed and sickly,
Edward succeeded at the age of nine. His uncle, the Duke of
Somerset, set aside the Council of Regency and established himself as
Protector of the realm, until his rival, the Duke of Northumberland,
engineered his downfall in 1549 and effectively took his place. A
rigorous Protestant himself, Edward actively encouraged the religious
developments of his reign. As he was manifestly frail by late 1552,
Northumberland devised the plot to safeguard Protestantism in
England and maintain his own position at the centre of power.
Edward, apparently with due consideration, signed the document to
alter the succession in favour of Lady Jane Grey. This portrait, of
about 1546, is the standard profile image of Edward.

29 MARY I 1516-58. Reigned 1553-8
By Hans Eworth, 1554

Only surviving child of Henry VIII and Catherine of Aragon, Mary's life was lonely and ultimately tragic. Devoted to her mother and to her mother's religion, she was heartbroken by the king's rejection of Catherine and embittered by Anne Boleyn's harsh treatment. Under the gentle influence of Catherine Parr, in 1544 Henry revised his will to allow Mary to succeed if Edward died childless. After the failure of Northumberland's plot, Mary, as queen, concentrated on the objectives most dear to her — the restoration of Roman Catholicism and her marriage. Thus she forfeited her considerable popularity and her reputation. Her proposal to marry Philip II of Spain caused widespread consternation and enabled Sir Thomas Wyatt to raise rebellion in Kent. However, the marriage was celebrated in 1554, when Philip made a brief visit to England. Mary's zealous restoration of the Roman Church led to the enforcement of laws against heretics, and hundreds of Reformers, including Cranmer and Bishops Latimer and Ridley, were burned at Smithfield. Her touching loyalty to Philip brought England into war against France, and Calais was lost. When Mary died in November 1558, pathetically mistaking her illness for signs of pregnancy, few mourned her. In this delicate portrait by Eworth, Mary wears the large pendant pearl that was a wedding present from Philip.

30 THOMAS WENTWORTH, 1st BARON WENTWORTH 1501-51
Attributed to John Bettes, 1549-50

Thomas Wentworth was in the king's service firstly as a soldier and later as a member of the royal household. He actively supported Henry's petition for divorce, and was one of the peers who tried and condemned Anne Boleyn. He became a Privy Councillor in 1549 and Lord Chamberlain in 1550. His portrait was begun in 1549, but not completed until early the next year. The picture was altered to take into account his increased status; the gloves were transferred from the left to the right hand and the white rod of office was inserted in their place.

A DÑ 1572
Æ · SVÆ · 3 2

VIRTVTIS · COMES · INVIDIA

HONI · SOIT · QVI · MAL · Y · PENSE

Opposite
31   WALTER DEVEREUX, 1st EARL OF ESSEX 1514?-76
By an unknown artist, 1572

Essex came to prominence in 1569, helping to suppress the northern rebellion. In 1573 he volunteered to colonize Ireland and bring it under English control, but his behaviour was excessively cruel, even by contemporary standards, and he was recalled. The occasion for this splendid portrait was his appointment as a Knight of the Garter in 1572 and his creation as Earl of Essex the same year. On the left, his coat of arms is encompassed by the Garter and surmounted by an earl's coronet.

THE ELIZABETHANS

The omens for what was to be one of the golden periods in British history did not look auspicious when Elizabeth ascended the throne in 1558. She inherited a nation weakened by political and religious conflicts, and a prey to pressures from more powerful neighbours. Elizabeth herself was a young woman inexperienced in affairs of state and beset by matrimonial offers. From the first, however, she showed herself to be a ruler of rare intelligence and ability. The Anglican settlement, though it satisfied neither Roman Catholics nor Puritans, appealed to a broad section of opinion, and established a secure church. Elizabeth united the nation around the figure of the Virgin Queen, who became a symbol of national resurgence. She dealt firmly with problems at home, conspiracies, and the perennial threat from Scotland, which was exacerbated by the overthrow of her cousin, Mary Queen of Scots.

Abroad she played off her powerful neighbours, keeping them guessing about her real intentions until she felt strong enough to resist them. It took Philip II of Spain thirty years to discover that England was one of the most implacable of his enemies, and unregenerately Protestant. The defeat of the Spanish Armada in 1588 was not only a great naval victory, but a vindication of Elizabeth's foreign policy of procrastination and prevarication. The conflict with Spain was intensified by commercial and colonial rivalry. For years English privateers raided the Spanish Main, seeking new opportunities for trade and expansion in the New World. Seamen like Drake and Hawkins represent the buccaneering and adventurous spirit of the Elizabethans. The growth of trade brought new wealth to the developing nation.

Elizabeth's court was a dazzling and scintillating one. Though noted for her parsimony, she dressed magnificently, and delighted in masques and spectacles. And the men she attracted to her service were dashing and talented, ministers like Burghley and Hatton, courtiers like Leicester and Essex, and poets and adventurers like Raleigh and Sidney. Under her patronage literature and the arts flourished as never before, giving us not only the greatest dramatist of the English-speaking world, William Shakespeare, but a host of lesser luminaries. Elizabethan art and music are elegant and exquisite. The jewelled miniatures by Nicholas Hilliard reflect a brilliant, shadowless world, with arabesque patterns, strange symbolic allusions, and vivid, heraldic colour. And the portraits in large by Anglo-Flemish artists like Marcus Gheeraerts are no less decorative and striking.

So numerous are the achievements of the age that it is difficult to summarize them. There was a feeling of excitement in the discovery of new worlds and new ideas that communicated itself in every sphere. The country prospered, intellectual and artistic life flowered. No wonder that during the troubled reigns of James I and Charles I people looked back nostalgically to the glorious days of Good Queen Bess.

45   ELIZABETH I 1533-1603. Reigned 1558-1603
By an unknown artist

Daughter of Anne Boleyn, Elizabeth's troubled childhood and vulnerable youth fostered talents of inestimable value to her as queen — caution, sound judgement and subterfuge. She survived to succeed Mary, and ruled for forty-four years. Her name has become synonymous with a period of political stability at home, decisive influence abroad and a dazzling, sophisticated court. Elizabeth appears here in her coronation robe of cloth of gold. This formal, full-face image, traditional for a royal portrait, was also used on coins, seals and official documents.

46 SIR WALTER RALEIGH 1552?-1618
By Nicholas Hilliard, c.1585

Poet, author and naval commander, Raleigh's handsome face, brilliant wit and charming manners captivated the queen. He was a particular favourite the 1580s, when this miniature was painted. His secret marriage to one o Elizabeth's ladies led to his disgrace.

Far left

47 SIR FRANCIS DRAKE 1540?-96
By Nicholas Hilliard, 1581

Drake was one of the sea captains w played a decisive role in the conflict against Spain on the high seas. This miniature was painted the year Drake returned from his voyage round the world, his ships richly laden with Spanish treasure.

Left

48 ROBERT DUDLEY, EARL OF LEICESTER 1532?-88
By Nicholas Hilliard, 1576

Of all Elizabeth's courtiers, Leicester was her undoubted favourite. The mysterious death of his first wife, An Robsart, and his arrogant assumption of influence over the queen made him unpopular. Leicester's haughty good looks are superbly portrayed in this miniature.

Bottom

49 ELIZABETH I 1533-1603. Reigned 1558-1603
By Nicholas Hilliard, 1572

This delicate portrait is the earliest of many surviving miniatures of Elizabeth by Hilliard. It was probably based on a sitting from life, sketched as described by Hilliard, 'where no tree was near, nor any shadow at all'. The white roses on her shoulder are a symbol of virginity.

50 SIR HENRY LEE 1533-1611
By Antonio Mor, 1568

Sir Henry Lee was Elizabeth's Master of the Ordnance and a key figure in the revival of the cult of chivalry at court. On 17 November 1559, anniversary of Elizabeth's accession day, he issued a challenge against all comers, and he maintained his role as Queen's Champion until 1590. He arranged the annual accession day tournaments which became ever more spectacular. While on official duties in Antwerp in 1568, Lee commissioned a portrait from Antonio Mor, Court Painter to Philip II of Spain. Steeped as he was in the imagery of chivalry and romance, the symbolism in his portrait (rings, and the armillary spheres on the sleeves) is not unexpected, though unfortunately never satisfactorily explained.

Below

51 WILLIAM CECIL, 1st LORD BURGHLEY 1520-98
Attributed to Arnold van Brounckhorst, c.1560-70

Elizabeth's unerring instinct for choosing the ablest men to serve her was never more in evidence than in her choice of Cecil as Secretary of State in 1558 and Lord High Treasurer from 1572. He was her principal adviser and most diligent minister for forty years, and his shrewd, trustworthy face appears in countless surviving portraits to reflect his pre-eminence at court. In this portrait, one of the earliest, he holds the Secretary's white staff of office.

53 SIR CHRISTOPHER HATTON 1540-91
By an unknown artist

As a young law student at the Inns of Court, Hatton's handsome face and figure, his skill as a dancer and prowess at the tournaments attracted Queen Elizabeth, and he rose rapidly to high favour. The miniaturist, Hilliard, described him as 'one of the goodliest personages of England, yet had he a very low forehead, not answerable to that good proportion of a third part of his face'. Although he had had little legal experience, he was appointed Lord Chancellor in 1587 and acquitted himself well. In his portrait, Hatton displays a cameo portrait of the queen, a convention which became popular among those in her service. He was perhaps the most devoted and sincere of her courtiers, for he never married.

52 ROBERT DUDLEY, EARL OF LEICESTER 1532?-88
By an unknown artist, c.1575

As son of the Duke of Northumberland, executed for
championing Lady Jane Grey, Leicester narrowly escaped
execution himself. His long friendship with Elizabeth I lasted
from her accession in 1558 until his death. He was her only
serious English suitor until Elizabeth realized that marriage to
him would be universally unpopular. In 1586 he led an
unsuccessful expedition to aid the Dutch in revolt against Spain,
and in 1588 was appointed to command the English army.
Leicester was an important patron of the arts and owned a large
collection of portraits. His personal vanity is reflected in the
dozen occasions he sat for his own portrait. This one is a typical
example of the Elizabethan style.

54 SIR HENRY UNTON 1557?-96
By an unknown artist, c.1596

A man of many talents, Sir Henry Unton died on a diplomatic
mission in France. This biographical picture, probably commissioned
by his widow, illustrates his main interests and achievements and
records the events immediately after his death. Reading from right to
left, Unton first appears as a baby in the arms of his mother,
formerly the Countess of Warwick. Above, he is shown studying at
Oxford University and then on his travels in Europe. Next (top
centre) he is in the Netherlands with Leicester's expedition, where he
was knighted. Immediately below are scenes in his house (see plate
55). Unton then appears on his death-bed, dying of a fever. His final
request to be buried in England is depicted below and on the left.
The skeleton (or skull) and hour-glass are recurrent symbols in Tudor
portraits as reminders of death. This picture is one of a very few
Tudor pictures showing scenes from everyday life.

55 SIR HENRY UNTON (detail from plate 54)
By an unknown artist

This scene (the exact occasion is not known) shows a banquet at
Wadley House. The feasters are being entertained by a masque, a
favourite Elizabethan diversion. The dancers are in fancy dress, led
in procession by Diana and Mercury. Lady Dorothy Unton, Sir
Henry's wife, is seated on the right.

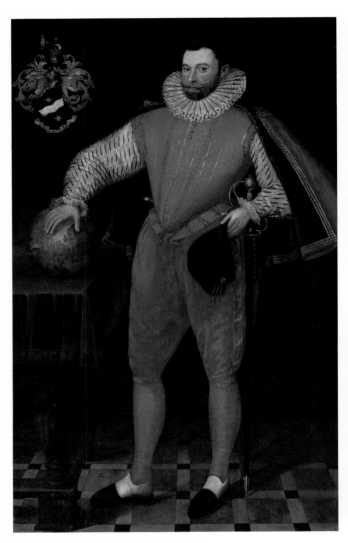

56   SIR FRANCIS DRAKE 1540?-96
By an unknown artist, c.1585

After three successful raiding expeditions to the West Indies,
Drake began his famous voyage round the world in 1577.
When he returned three years later, laden with Spanish
treasure, Philip II of Spain demanded that he should be
punished. Instead, Elizabeth knighted him. By now Drake's
daring and resourcefulness had become legendary, as had his
violent temper, unscrupulousness and conceit. In 1587, as
Philip was preparing his navy for invasion, Drake sailed into
Cadiz harbour with thirty small ships and set fire to the fleet.
This postponed the Armada for a year and gave England a
chance to prepare for the attack. He was second-in-command
of the English navy in 1588 and played a decisive role in the
Armada's defeat, although his proposition to engage the
Spaniards in battle before they reached the Channel had been
disregarded. His last expedition to the West Indies in 1595
was unsuccessful, and he died there of dysentery. This rare
whole-length panel may have been worked up from a head
and shoulders portrait.

57   SIR PHILIP SIDNEY 1554-86
By an unknown artist, after a portrait of 1577

Sidney was the model Elizabethan hero. As Elizabeth's envoy to the
Netherlands, he was an ardent champion of the Protestant cause
and gained the admiration of William the Silent and the Dutch nobles
in rebellion against Catholic Spanish control in the Netherlands. He
became Governor of Flushing in 1585 and joined his uncle, the Earl
of Leicester, on the expedition in 1586 to aid the Dutch. Fatally
wounded at the Battle of Zutphen, he died soon afterwards. Sidney
was a cultivated Renaissance man of letters, a friend and patron of
poets and a poet himself. His famous collection of love sonnets
known as *Astrophel and Stella* and his prose romance *Arcadia* were
written in the early 1580s. In this portrait, Sidney appears as a young
soldier of twenty-three.

AMOR ET VIRTUTE.

ÆTATIS SVÆ 34
AN 1588

58   SIR WALTER RALEIGH 1552?-1618
Attributed to the monogrammist 'H'

Raleigh's first voyage of discovery to the West Indies was in 1578. In 1584 he established a short-lived settlement in North America, named Virginia. He was supplanted in Elizabeth's affections by young Essex and later banished from court for his clandestine relationship with Elizabeth Throckmorton. In 1595 he first sailed to the Orinoco in search of gold. Found guilty of treason by James I in 1603, he was released from prison in 1617 to lead another expedition to the Orinoco. This was a failure; he tangled with the Spaniards, his son was killed, and Raleigh's execution was demanded and obtained by Spain.

29

**59 ROBERT DEVEREUX, 2nd EARL OF
ESSEX 1566-1601**
By Marcus Gheeraerts the Younger, c.1597

Essex came to court in 1585, aged eighteen,
handsome and charming, under the protection
of his step-father, Leicester. Elizabeth was
immediately captivated, and, despite his
impudence towards other established favourites,
she indulged his whims. He soon distinguished
himself as a soldier and acquired an insatiable
taste for command and glory. Desperately
ambitious, he overestimated the extent to which
the doting queen would allow him to meddle in
state politics. As his demands were thwarted he
became more rash: 'a man of nature not to be
ruled'. His high-handed behaviour as Governor-
General of Ireland in 1599 finally exhausted the
queen's patience and he was imprisoned. Failing
to restore himself to favour, he became involved
in a plot against Elizabeth's ministers and tried
to raise rebellion in London. When this failed,
he was executed for treason. This portrait was
once at Ditchley, the house of Essex's friend, Sir
Henry Lee. Essex wears the robes of a Knight of
the Garter.

60 ELIZABETH I 1533-1603. Reigned 1558-1603
By Marcus Gheeraerts the Younger, c.1592

This magnificent portrait was commissioned by Sir Henry Lee (see plate 50) to
commemorate the queen's visit to Ditchley in 1592. Lee devised a spectacular
entertainment in her honour, in which she took part. This is the image of Gloriana,
ageless, indomitable and triumphant. Elizabeth personifies England; she has guided
the realm through the dangerous storms of war into the golden sunlight of peace.
'When she smiled it was pure sunshine that everyone did choose to bask in, if they
could; but anon came a storm from a sudden gathering of clouds and the thunder
fell in wondrous manner on all alike.' The sonnet in the picture, almost certainly by
Lee, describes her as the 'Prince of Light'. The map she stands on (her feet on
Ditchley, Lee's Oxfordshire country seat) was published by John Saxton in 1583.

61 SIR THOMAS CONINGSBY 1551-1625
Attributed to George Gower, 1572

This portrait of the soldier Sir Thomas Coningsby shows him with the accoutrements of falconry. He holds the falcon's hood in one hand and swings the lure with the other. The Latin and Italian inscriptions suggest an allegory comparing the bird to youth. The town in the background may represent Coningsby's native city, Hereford. Allegories and symbols were as popular in Elizabethan portraits as they were in contemporary literature.

62 MARY THROCKMORTON, LADY SCUDAMORE d.1632
By Marcus Gheeraerts the Younger, c.1614

The sitter has recently been identified as Lady Scudamore. The date and inscription refer to the marriage of her son John to Elizabeth Porter in March 1614. This masterpiece of early English painting adopts many typical elements of Jacobean portraiture, such as the draped curtain and the hand resting on a table. However, it is unusual for the figure to be shown in such an informal manner. The black-work embroidery is a particularly fine example of Gheeraert's controlled and detailed brushwork.

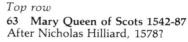

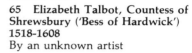

Top row

63   Mary Queen of Scots 1542-87
After Nicholas Hilliard, 1578?

64   Sir Richard Bingham 1528-99
By an unknown artist, 1564

Second row

65   Elizabeth Talbot, Countess of Shrewsbury ('Bess of Hardwick') 1518-1608
By an unknown artist

66   Sir Thomas Gresham 1519?-79
By an unknown Flemish artist, c.1565

67   Sir Richard Grenville 1541?-91
By an unknown artist, after a portrait of 1571

68   Sir Edward Hoby 1560-1617
By an unknown artist, 1583

Third row

69   Sir Nicholas Throckmorton 1515-71
By an unknown artist, c.1562

70   Charles Howard, 1st Earl of Nottingham, Lord High Admiral 1536-1624
By an unknown artist, 1602

Bottom

71   George Clifford, 3rd Earl of Cumberland 1558-1605
After Nicholas Hilliard

72   CHARLES I 1600-49. Reigned 1625-49
By Gerard Honthorst, 1628

In this surprisingly informal portrait of the young king reading, the Dutch artist Honthorst expresses the serious-minded, contemplative side of Charles's character — the scholar and connoisseur, rather than the monarch. Honthorst was in London at the king's invitation between April and December 1628, and the portrait was almost certainly painted at this time, as an *ad*

vivum study for the artist's *Apollo and Diana*. This huge allegorical canvas, commissioned by the king, now hangs on the Queen's Staircase at Hampton Court. In it Charles is shown as Apollo and the queen as Diana, while the Duke of Buckingham appears as Mercury presenting the Seven Liberal Arts to the king. As a reward Charles created Honthorst an English citizen and gave him munificent presents, including three thousand guilders and a lifetime pension of a hundred pounds a year.

CAVALIERS AND ROUNDHEADS

On 30 January 1649, on a scaffold erected in front of Inigo Jones's Banqueting House in Whitehall, Charles I was beheaded. This last brutal act of the Civil War was the culmination of the political disintegration of the monarchy and of its prestige which had begun with Charles's father, James I. It brought to an end what was in many ways the most civilized court in Europe; it dashed for ever the doctrine of the Divine Right of Kings, and at the same time made possible the transition to modern Parliamentary government.

The origins of this break-up can be traced to the personality of James I, who, ironically, when he succeeded to the throne of England in 1603 was seen as bringing welcome stability after the uncertainty of Elizabeth I's last years. James's personality was fatally flawed by his early years as child king of Scotland, when he had been the puppet of warring political factions. Feelings of insecurity and suspicion never left him; he was fiercely autocratic, extravagant, learned but pedantic, with a penchant for handsome but often ill-chosen favourites. From his father, Charles inherited his extravagance, his aloof manner, and above all that most dangerous of favourites, the Duke of Buckingham. Buckingham's misconceived schemes ruined Charles's relationship with Parliament, but it was Charles's own ineptitude in political matters and his refusal to deal directly with Parliament which finally brought civil war to England.

From the chaos of war emerged the military genius of Oliver Cromwell, whose status as a popular leader was, however, irreparably damaged by the execution of Charles. He proved unable to establish a formula by which he could govern the country with the support of Parliament. The Protectorship became a military dictatorship, and it was this failure which ultimately led to the restoration of the monarchy.

Throughout this period of political unrest the arts, by contrast, flourished. In their different ways both James and Charles were outstanding patrons of the arts, as were courtiers such as the Earl of Arundel and the Duke of Buckingham. James and his consort Anne of Denmark indulged their taste for the exotic through elaborately artificial court masques, written by Ben Jonson and staged with spectacular costumes and scenery by Inigo Jones. From Jones the Banqueting House and the Queen's House at Greenwich were commissioned. Peake, De Critz, Mytens and Van Somer and the miniaturists Hilliard and Oliver painted the king and his court. It was the greatest age of the English commercial theatre, when Shakespeare wrote his mature plays and Jonson his comedies. At the same time, in the sciences Sir Francis Bacon was testing by experiment notions which had been accepted uncritically for hundreds of years, and William Harvey, physician to Charles I, was soon to begin the experiments which established the principle of the circulation of the blood.

Love of the arts was Charles I's ruling passion. For him Rubens adorned the ceiling of the Banqueting House with huge allegorical canvases glorifying James I, while his agents scoured Europe for the greatest classical and Renaissance works of art with which to adorn his palaces. He lavishly patronized living artists, and above all Van Dyck, for whom he had a profound admiration. It is largely through Van Dyck's eyes and the eyes of the artists influenced by him that we see Charles's courtiers — the cavaliers — in their easy yet elegant dress, their faces touched with a faint air of melancholy. It was a generation which, along with the king and his collections, the Civil War destroyed.

73   JAMES I 1566-1625. Reigned 1603-25
By Daniel Mytens, 1621

The son of Mary Queen of Scots and Lord Darnley, and great-great-grandson of Henry VII, James succeeded to the Scottish throne while still a baby, on the abdication of his mother in 1567. In 1603 he succeeded Elizabeth I on the English throne, thus uniting England and Scotland. With a taste for unpopular favourites and in constant fear of assassination, he was undignified in appearance and conduct. Inclined to pedantry, he yet wrote poetry and encouraged spectacular theatricals at court. By his unshakeable belief in the Divine Right of Kings he nurtured the quarrel with Parliament which ultimately destroyed Charles I. To contemporaries he appeared 'naturally of a timorous disposition...his eye large, ever rowling after any stranger came in his presence...his Beard was very thin...his legs were very weak...his walk ever circular'. In Mytens's superficially grand portrait of him in the splendid robes of the Order of the Garter, James seems dwarfed by his trappings, and his expression betrays unease. Prominent in the tapestry behind him is a Tudor rose and the motto *Beati Pacifici*, 'Blessed are the peace-makers'.

74   HENRY, PRINCE OF WALES 1594-1612
By Robert Peake the Elder, c.1610

Prince Henry was the talented eldest son of James I and Anne of Denmark. He came to represent the perfect young Renaissance prince — good-looking, learned, pious, skilled in arms, and with an appreciative understanding of the arts. His early death from typhoid fever, only two years after he had been created Prince of Wales, was a heavy blow to national morale. In Peake's brilliantly coloured and intricately patterned portrait, the pose of the precocious sixteen-year-old is one of absolute assurance. He wears the Garter and Jewel of the Order of the Garter, while on the table is his splendid plumed hat with a jewel formed of the letters HP, standing for *Henricus Princeps*. The Prince of Wales's feathers are used as a motif in the embroidery on the edge of the table-cloth, while the unusual landscape vista is perhaps intended to show the park at Richmond which the prince had altered and extended.

75 THE SOMERSET HOUSE CONFERENCE, 1604
By an unknown artist, 1604

This rare group-portrait of an actual historical event commemorates the treaty of peace and trade between England and Spain, signed at Hampton Court on 16 August 1604, which ended almost twenty years of war. The representatives of Spain and the Catholic Netherlands are seated on the left of the table; on the right the English delegates: the Earls of Dorset, Nottingham, Devonshire and Northampton, and, nearest the spectator, Robert Cecil, Viscount Cranborne, Secretary of State.

76 ANNE OF DENMARK 1574-1619
By Isaac Oliver, c.1610

Anne was the daughter of Frederick II of Denmark, and married James I in 1589. Of the seven children she bore him, only three survived infancy. She was fond of hunting and of progresses. For her Inigo Jones designed the Queen's House at Greenwich, and with Ben Jonson created the lavish and fantastic court masques in which she delighted to perform. Oliver's miniature lovingly details the queen's rich dress and some of her favourite jewels.

Right

77 THOMAS HOWARD, 2nd EARL OF ARUNDEL AND SURREY 1586-1646
By Sir Peter Paul Rubens, 1629

Arundel was the outstanding collector-connoisseur of his generation. Patron of living artists like Inigo Jones, Van Dyck and Rubens, he also formed a magnificent collection of old master paintings and drawings, and brought together the 'Arundel marbles', now in Oxford. Rubens called him 'an evangelist in the world of art'. His penetrating portrait is a study for the threequarter-length painting in the Isabella Stewart Gardner Museum, Boston.

78 WILLIAM SHAKESPEARE 1564-1616
By an unknown artist, c.1610

Appropriately, this portrait of arguably the world's greatest dramatist was the first picture to be acquired by the National Portrait Gallery, presented by the Earl of Ellesmere in 1856. Known as the 'Chandos portrait', after the 3rd Duke of Chandos, a former owner, it is the only portrait in oils of Shakespeare to have any claim to authenticity. In the late seventeenth century it was said to have been painted by one John Taylor, 'a Player, who acted for Shakespeare'.

79 BEN JONSON 1573?-1637
By Abraham van Blijenberch, c.1618

The greatest English dramatist of the neo-classical tradition, Jonson, in his satirical comedies *Every Man in his Humour* (in which Shakespeare acted), *Volpone* and *The Alchemist*, combines classical notions of structure and unity with a ready intellectual wit and lyric charm. With Inigo Jones he produced a series of spectacular masques for the court, often based on abstruse allegories. He was naturally belligerent, and was described by John Aubrey as having 'one eie lower then t'other and bigger'.

38

80   JOHN EVELYN 1620-1706
By Robert Walker, 1648

Evelyn records in his celebrated *Diary* that he sat to
Walker on 1 July 1648. He poses in melancholy
attitude, meditating on death. The Greek inscription
means 'Repentance is the beginning of wisdom', and
his paper is inscribed with a quotation from Seneca on
the importance of preparing for death.

Above
81   WILLIAM HARVEY 1578-1657
By an unknown artist, c.1627

This portrait, known as the 'Rolls Park portrait' from
the house where it was discovered in 1948, is the only
one surviving to show Harvey in his prime — a year
before he published *De Motu Cordis et Sanguinis*. In
this he established his epoch-making discovery, based
on years of practical experiment, of the principle of
the circulation of the bood. Harvey was physician to
Charles I and the leading anatomist of his day. Even
in this unambitious canvas, something of his
penetrating intellectual curiosity shines out.

82   JOHN MILTON 1608-74
By an unknown artist, c.1629

This portrait of the twenty-one-year-old poet is
probably that mentioned by John Aubrey: 'His
widowe has his picture drawne very well & like when
a Cambridge schollar. He was so faire that they called
him the Lady of Christ's coll'. It is an unexpected
image of the man better known as the formidably
learned author of the epics *Paradise Lost* and *Paradise
Regained*, and the tragedy *Samson Agonistes*; the
political pamphleteer and polemicist who became
Cromwell's Latin Secretary.

83 THE FAMILY OF ARTHUR, 1st LORD CAPEL (1604-49)

By Cornelius Johnson, c.1639

Capel was a devoted royalist, who suffered for his loyalty, dying on the scaffold. This portrait of him with his wife Elizabeth, from the years before the Civil War, is Johnson's attempt at a group portrait in the manner of Van Dyck. His work lacks Van Dyck's assurance and elegance, but has a touching naivety and a devotion to details of dress which are peculiarly his. The children are Arthur, later 1st Earl of Essex; Charles; Henry, later Lord Capel of Tewkesbury; Elizabeth, later Countess of Carnarvon; and Mary, later Duchess of Beaufort. The gardens behind are perhaps those of Little Hadham, Capel's home. Elizabeth was a talented botanical artist, Mary became a distinguished horticulturalist, and Henry established a garden at Kew.

84 THOMAS WENTWORTH, 1st EARL OF STRAFFORD 1593-1641

Studio of Sir Anthony van Dyck, 1636

Wentworth was a statesman of severe and ruthless methods, yet with a belief in the power of responsible government under the Crown. Initially of the Parliamentary party, he was won over by Charles I, becoming President of the Council of the North in 1628, and in 1632 Lord Deputy in Ireland, where he restored order by the policy called 'Thorough'. He returned to England in 1639, convinced of the need for absolute authority, and urging strong measures on Charles. But his policies were defeated on all sides. Despite Charles's promise to protect him, he was impeached by the Long Parliament and executed. His powerful personality is preserved in a series of magnificent portraits by Van Dyck.

85 ARCHBISHOP WILLIAM LAUD 1573-1645
By an unknown artist after Sir Anthony van Dyck, c.1636?

Laud was Charles I's influential and devoted Archbishop of Canterbury. A passionately sincere High Churchman and an implacable enemy of Puritanism, he carried out Strafford's policy of 'Thorough' in ecclesiastical matters. He enforced ritualism and uniformity in church services in England, and attempted to impose the English Prayer Book on Scotland, thus raising the Covenanters and leading to the Bishops' Wars. Like his associate, Strafford, Laud by his authoritarianism deprived himself of all popular support, and was impeached by the Long Parliament in 1640. He was executed four years later. Van Dyck's original portrait hangs at Lambeth Palace. In October 1640 Laud found it 'fallen down upon the face...the string being broken...God grant this be no omen!'

86 GEORGE VILLIERS, 1st DUKE OF BUCKINGHAM (1592-1628) AND HIS FAMILY
By an unknown artist after Gerard Honthorst, 1628

The original of this idyllic family group, now at Buckingham Palace, was painted by Honthorst sometime between his arrival in England in April 1628 and August, when Buckingham was assassinated by a fanatic, John Felton, in Portsmouth. Buckingham was an ambitious but incompetent favourite, whom Charles I inherited from his father James I. In 1623 he had travelled with Charles to Spain to arrange a marriage with the Spanish Infanta, and when negotiations failed he hurried James into war with Spain. His bungling of the expeditions to Cadiz and La Rochelle made him immensely unpopular, Parliament's 'grievance of grievances', and he did much to accelerate the deterioration of Charles's relations with Parliament.

87   THE FIVE ELDEST CHILDREN OF CHARLES I
By an unknown artist after Sir Anthony van Dyck, 1637

A copy of Van Dyck's touching family group at Windsor Castle, which
originally hung in Charles I's Breakfast Chamber at Whitehall. The sitters are
(left to right): Princess Mary (1631-60), later Princess of Orange, mother of
William III; James, Duke of York, later James II; Charles, later Charles II;
Princess Elizabeth (1635-50); and Princess Anne (1636-40). Van Dyck asked
£200 for the picture, reduced to £100 by Charles. The group was immediately
popular, and its effect is well described by a later painter, Sir David Wilkie:
'the simplicity of inexperience shows them in most engaging contrast with the
power of their rank and station, and like the infantas of Velasquez, unites all
the demure stateliness of the court, with the perfect artlessness of childhood'.

88   ELIZABETH, QUEEN OF BOHEMIA 1596-1662
From the studio of Gerard Honthorst, c.1642

The beautiful and vivacious eldest daughter of James I, Elizabeth married in
1613 Frederick, staunchly Protestant Elector of the Palatinate. In 1619,
against the counsel of most of his advisers, but boldly supported by his rash
wife, he accepted the crown of Bohemia from the Protestant anti-Habsburg
party. He was, however, driven from the throne by the Austrians only a
year later, an incident which touched off the Thirty Years War. In the
following years Elizabeth lived as a fugitive — the legendary 'Winter Queen',
who roused in England a deep romantic sympathy. After the Restoration she
returned here to live with her favourite son, Prince Rupert. Her daughter
Sophia, wife of the Elector of Hanover, was the mother of George I.

89 HENRIETTA MARIA 1609-69
By an unknown artist, the background probably by Hendrik van Steenwyck the Younger, c.1635?

Henrietta Maria, the youngest daughter of Henry IV of France, married Charles I in 1625. Although at first relations with her husband were strained, they later enjoyed a happy family life. The queen was headstrong and Catholic, and her interventions in politics did much to damage her husband's cause. She fled to France in 1644, and did not return until the Restoration. She is immortalized in her many portraits by Van Dyck, and this grand whole-length is painted in a simplified version of Van Dyck's manner. Sophia of Bavaria, who saw the queen in 1641, wrote: 'I was surprised to find that the Queen, who looked so fine in painting, was a small woman raised up on her chair, with long skinny arms and teeth like defence works projecting from her mouth'.

90 CHARLES I 1600-49. Reigned 1625-49
Studio of Daniel Mytens, 1631

This somewhat muted whole-length was painted when Charles was thirty-one, after two years of his eleven-year period of personal government without Parliament. The crown, sceptre and orb on the table emphasize the king's temporal power, while a now almost illegible inscription on the balustrade to his left proclaims him King of Great Britain, France and Scotland, and Defender of the Faith. Although conceived as a great state portrait, of which numerous official versions were distributed, Mytens's work has a direct, unrhetorical quality which conveys something of Charles's gentle and courteous nature. The slight stiffness of pose is a reminder that only a year later Van Dyck was to arrive in London and to revolutionize the portraiture of Charles and his court, with his sheer technical brilliance, elegance and sense of poetry.

91 CHARLES I (1600-49; reigned 1625-49) AND SIR EDWARD WALKER (1612-77)
By an unknown artist, after 1647

This unusual double portrait of the king campaigning was perhaps commissioned by his companion Sir Edward Walker, the proud and quarrelsome Garter King-at-Arms. One of the engagements — possibly at Winchester — in the West Country campaigns of 1644-5 may be illustrated in the background. The artist has adapted the figure of the king from Lely's portrait of him with James, Duke of York (1647) at Syon House.

92 PRINCE RUPERT 1619-82
Attributed to Gerard Honthorst, c.1641-2

The third son of Frederick of the Palatinate and Elizabeth of Bohemia, Rupert's early years were overshadowed by the troubles of his parents. In the Civil War, in support of his uncle Charles I, he was first a reckless and brilliant cavalry leader, and later fought at sea. At the Restoration he fought in the Dutch Wars. He founded the Hudson Bay Company in 1670, and was interested in scientific experiment.

93 OLIVER CROMWELL 1599-1658
By Robert Walker, c.1649

Charles I's great antagonist was the son of a Huntingdon country gentleman, and entered Parliament in 1628. His military genius, first shown at Edgehill, sustained his career, and the New Model Army which he had formed was the chief single factor in winning the Civil War. By the army he was led to overthrow Parliament and take office as Protector. Appropriately, Walker shows Cromwell in armour, holding his commander's baton, but he smooths over the 'ruffness, pimples, warts & everything' which Cromwell had demanded of another painter.

45

GENERAL MONK

94   GEORGE MONCK, 1st DUKE OF ALBEMARLE 1608-70
Studio of Sir Peter Lely, 1665-6

This portrait is a version of one in the series of 'Flagmen', commissioned by James, Duke of York, and now at the National Maritime Museum. It commemorates his command after the Restoration as an admiral in the Dutch wars. Monck's earlier career is marked by political pragmatism fortified by great personal integrity. Initially a royalist, he turned, after two years in the Tower, to Parliament, and under Cromwell held command in both Scotland and Ireland. On Cromwell's death he led his army from Scotland to London, demanding nothing but a 'free Parliament' — the Convention Parliament which restored the monarchy and made him a duke.

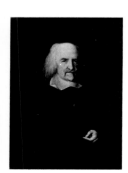

THE RESTORATION AND
THE GLORIOUS REVOLUTION

With the eagerly acclaimed restoration of Charles II in 1660 England once more had its monarchy. The new king was easy-going and, as he admitted himself, 'more lazy than I ought to be', but he brought with him all the splendour of monarchy, and was surrounded by a court which expressed in its dress, manners and morals the feeling of release after the anxieties of the Civil War and the restraint of the Interregnum. It was a brilliant society, epitomized by the group of beautiful and audacious royal mistresses, of whom the witty comedienne Nell Gwyn was the most notorious.

Charles's policies reflected his personality: he was by temperament an absolutist, and was strongly influenced by Louix XIV of France. Not a deeply religious man, he favoured religious toleration, in particular for Roman Catholics, and proclaimed his own Roman Catholicism on his deathbed. By exercising tact and discretion he avoided political disaster, but he never succeeded in implementing his pro-Catholic and pro-French policies.

It was Catholicism which fatally blighted the reign of Charles's younger brother, James II. Lacking his brother's tact, James rapidly alienated an initially friendly Parliament and the bulk of his supporters by his intensely pro-Catholic policies and appointments, and made inevitable the revolution of 1688. Only with the invitation to William of Orange and his wife Mary (James's daughter) to take the throne of England on terms which assured the ascendancy of the British Parliamentary and party system, was the Protestant succession finally secured.

Whatever Charles II's weaknesses of character, he showed a lively interest in the arts and sciences. He patronized a wide range of British and foreign artists, as did his fashion-conscious mistresses. Grinling Gibbons adorned his palaces with exquisite wood-carving; Sir Christopher Wren was Surveyor General of the King's Works; Henry Purcell, one of the most original of all English composers, was organist of the Chapel Royal and Keeper of the King's Instruments. Charles encouraged the foundation of the Royal Society, and it was he who in 1662 gave it its first charter, thus providing a focus and means of recognition for the work of such men as Wren (who was a gifted mathematician as well as an architect), Robert Boyle and Sir Isaac Newton, and many more. He was an enthusiastic theatre-goer, and the dramatist, satirist and critic John Dryden was his Poet Laureate. The flourishing cultural atmosphere which he helped to stimulate has had an influence far beyond his reign: the German artist Kneller, for instance, who first sought patronage at Charles's court, lived to paint George I, and has captured for all time the baroque exuberance of the full-bottomed wig; Wren's masterpiece, St Paul's Cathedral, was not completed until the reign of Queen Anne, and, with his many other churches, it transformed the face of London; from the Restoration comedies by Dryden and Wycherley in which Charles delighted developed the comic masterpieces of Congreve; they later inspired Sheridan and Wilde, and are still enjoyed today.

108   CHARLES II 1630-85. Reigned 1660-85
By Edward Hawker, c. 1680-5?

This grand state portrait, by the obscure artist Edward Hawker, almost certainly shows Charles towards the very end of his reign. Awkwardly posed, he seems ill at ease amongst the trappings of the baroque portrait — voluminous curtains, ornate throne and rich robes and mantle, and his face is tired, speaking of years of insecurity and personal indulgence, but not without a trace of the tolerant good humour which made him popular with his subjects.

109 FRANCES JENNINGS, DUCHESS OF TYRCONNEL 1647/9-1731
By Samuel Cooper, c.1665

Samuel Cooper, 'the prince of limners of this age', as John Aubrey called him, and probably the greatest native English artist of the seventeenth century, has captured in the tiny space of a miniature the youthful beauty's enchanting colouring and expression. She was the elder sister of Sarah Jennings, later Duchess of Marlborough, and maid-of-honour at the court of Charles II. A contemporary wrote of her: 'Miss Jennings, arrayed in all the splendour of her first youth, had a complexion more dazzlingly fair than had ever yet been seen. Her tresses were a perfect blonde; but there was something about her so vivid and animated that it guaranteed her general colouring against that sort of insipidity which is usually associated with extreme fairness. Her mouth was not of the smallest, but it was the best-shaped mouth in the world...the turn of her face was delightful, and her bosom...was of the same brilliance of her complexion'. The miniature is laid on a highly decorated mount, probably of the eighteenth century.

110 LOUISE RENÉE DE PENANCOET DE KÉROUALLE, DUCHESS OF PORTSMOUTH 1649-1734
By Pierre Mignard, 1682

The duchess first came to England in 1670 as maid-of-honour to Henrietta, Duchess of Orleans, and shortly afterwards was sent back to England by Louis XIV to win the king to her heart and to the French interest. This she achieved, becoming Charles II's mistress in 1671. She subsequently bore a son, later Duke of Richmond, and was herself created duchess in 1673. John Evelyn noted her 'childish, simple and baby face', and her lavish apartments in Whitehall, which had 'ten times the richnesse & glory beyond the Queenes'. She popularized French fashions and taste at court, but was hated by the people. After Charles's death she returned to France, and Voltaire, who saw her in old age, paid tribute to her beauty. In this portrait she is presented with coral, pearls and a shell by her negro page, and is perhaps portrayed as the sea-nymph Thetis, mother of the hero Achilles — an allusion to her son by Charles.

111 CATHERINE OF BRAGANZA 1638-1705
By or after Dirk Stoop, c.1660-1

The daughter of John, Duke of Braganza, afterwards king of
Portugal, Catherine came to England as Charles II's bride in 1662,
bringing with her a welcome dowry of Bombay, Tangier and
£300,000. John Evelyn describes her arrival in England, and her
curious Portuguese costume: 'The Queene arived, with a traine of
Portugueze Ladys in their monstrous fardingals or Guard-Infantas:
Their complexions olivaster, & sufficiently unagreable: Her majestie
in the same habit, her foretop long & turned aside very strangely:
She was yet of the handsomest Countenance of all the rest, & tho
low of stature pretily shaped, languishing & excellent Eyes, her
teeth wronging her mouth by stiking a little too far out: for the rest
sweete & lovely enough'. The wide hooped skirt and odd looped
hair-style can be seen in Stoop's charming portrait, and a tradition
exists that it was a version of this portrait which was sent to
England, prior to her marriage, for Charles to inspect. She was a
shy and somewhat solemn girl, and devoted to her husband, who,
though he wounded her by his continuous infidelity, yet had a
genuine affection for her.

112 NELL GWYN 1650-87
Studio of Sir Peter Lely, c.1675

Nell Gwyn was the mistress of Charles II *par excellence,* and an
ebullient symbol of the licentious freedoms of the Restoration
court. Unlike her Catholic rival, the Duchess of Portsmouth,
she enjoyed great popularity: 'the Protestant whore', as she
herself said, and Pepys's 'bold merry slut'. Born in Hereford,
she rose from being an orange-seller at the Theatre Royal,
Drury Lane, to become one of the leading comic actresses of
her day — 'pretty witty Nell', and a king's mistress. Dryden
kept her supplied with a series of somewhat saucy, bustling
parts which ideally suited her talents, and Pepys thought her
outstanding as Florimel in Dryden's *The Maiden Queen.* But
this 'clever buffoon...played the part on and off the boards',
and was fond of mimicking members of the court, especially
her rival the Duchess of Portsmouth. Nell bore the king two
sons (the elder of whom was created Duke of St Albans), and
retained his favour until the end of his life. She died young of
an apoplectic fit. Lely shows her, not as the brilliant comic
actress, but in the highly fashionable guise of a shepherdess
with a lamb, the symbol of her innocence!

113   JAMES II (1633-1701; reigned 1685-8) AND ANNE HYDE (1637-71) AS DUKE AND DUCHESS OF YORK
By Sir Peter Lely, c.1660

This double portrait was probably painted shortly after James's secret marriage to the pregnant Anne Hyde. Her father Edward Hyde, later Earl of Clarendon, strongly disapproved of the match, but Charles II thought his sister-in-law 'a woman of great wit and excellent parts'. Pepys declared that 'the Duke of York, in all things but his amours, is led by the nose by his wife', but she did not live to be queen. Her daughters Mary and Anne both succeeded to the throne.

114   JOHN MAITLAND, 1st DUKE OF LAUDERDALE 1616-82
By Samuel Cooper, 1664

Bishop Burnet gave a brilliant sketch of this formidable politician: 'very big; his hair red, hanging oddly about him; his tongue was too big for his mouth, which made him bedew all that he talked to'. Cooper, in an equally small space, creates an almost palpable physical presence for this ruthless, unattractive but highly educated member of the Cabal, who at the Restoration became almost absolute ruler in Scotland. Ham House, at Richmond, remains as a monument to his genuine love of the arts.

115 GEORGE JEFFREYS, 1st BARON JEFFREYS 1645-89
Attributed to William Claret, c.1678-80

Jeffreys's name is for ever associated with the so-called 'Bloody Assize' of 1685, at which, as James II's Lord Chief Justice, he savagely punished the rebels who had followed the Duke of Monmouth. Three hundred and twenty were executed. This portrait, however, shows the energetic lawyer with a talent for cross-examination at an earlier stage of his career, about 1678, when he was appointed Recorder of London. The paper in Jeffreys's hand is inscribed 'Senatus Populusque Londiniensis', 'The Senate and People of London', and stresses this connection. After the Glorious Revolution of 1688 Jeffreys was captured and imprisoned in the Tower, where he died.

Below right

116 JAMES SCOTT, DUKE OF MONMOUTH AND BUCCLEUCH 1649-85
By an unknown artist probably after William Wissing, c.1683

Monmouth was the son of Charles II by Lucy Walter, 'a brown, beautiful, bold but insipid creature', as Pepys described her. To judge from his portrait, some of these characteristics were inherited by her son. Charles doted on the boy, and advanced his military career. But he became the focus of powerful Protestant forces opposed to the Roman Catholic Duke of York, and on James's accession he raised a rebellion and claimed the throne. He and his virtually peasant army were defeated at Sedgemoor. Monmouth fled before the battle was over, but was captured later and beheaded on Tower Hill.

117 JAMES II (1633-1701; reigned 1685-8) AS DUKE OF YORK
By Sir Peter Lely, c.1665-70

This masterly oil sketch by the greatest painter of the Restoration court is a vivid record of the encounter between the artist and a highly important sitter. The breadth and rapidity with which the hair and background are laid in implies that the sitting was short. Lely's powers are wonderfully concentrated here, and he creates a penetrating likeness with great economy of means.

118   SAMUEL PEPYS 1633-1703
By John Hayls, 1666

Although a naval administrator of great ability, who eventually
became Secretary of the Admiralty, Pepys is remembered above
all for the *Diary* which he began on 1 January 1660, and which he
laid aside in 1669, when he believed he was going blind. It is a
unique social document and piece of self-revelation, written in
code and only deciphered and published in 1825. His portrait is
documented in the *Diary*. Pepys first sat, wearing an Indian gown
which he had specially hired, on 17 March 1666: 'I... do almost
break my neck looking over my shoulders to make the posture for
him [Hayls] to work by', and on 16 May he paid Hayls £14 for
the completed portrait and twenty-five shillings for the frame. He
declared himself 'very well satisfied' with the portrait, in which he
holds a song, *Beauty retire, thou*, which he had himself set to
music.

Above right
119   SIR CHRISTOPHER WREN 1632-1723
By Sir Godfrey Kneller, 1711

This remarkable portrait by the German artist Kneller, with its
assured pose and confident expression, is a noble representation of
England's greatest architect. It was no doubt intended to
commemorate the completion in 1711 of Wren's masterpiece, St
Paul's Cathedral, for on the table lies a plan of the west end of the
cathedral. It comes as something of a shock to learn that in that
year Wren was seventy-nine years old, for his appearance is that
of a much younger man. He holds in his hands a pair of
compasses and on the plan rests a copy of Euclid, reminders that
the man who rebuilt London's churches after the Great Fire was
also one of the greatest geometers of the day and a former
Professor of Astronomy. He was President of the Royal Society
from 1680 to 1682, and an intimate of the greatest scientists and
thinkers of his time.

121 SIR ISAAC NEWTON 1642-1727
By Sir Godfrey Kneller, 1702

The plague years of 1665-6, and the enforced absence from
Cambridge which they entailed for him, were the time of the
greatest flowering of Newton's genius. In this short period, at
home at Woolsthorpe in Lincolnshire, he discovered the theory of
light and colours, attempted to verify his hypothesis of universal
gravitation, and generalized his calculus of fluxions. On this early
work alone, his reputation as one of the world's greatest scientists
would be secure. His research into optics brought him fame, and a
high place in society, but he felt that success had made him a
'slave to philosophy', so that he published unwillingly: his
Principia Mathematica in 1687 and the *Optics* in 1704. He was
President of the Royal Society for twenty-five years before his
death.

122 THE HON ROBERT BOYLE 1627-91
By an unknown artist after Johann Kerseboom, c.1689-90

Boyle is a classic example of the type of gentleman-amateur who
did so much to advance the scientific revolution in England. His
early interest in science was stimulated by the Grand Tour, and
consolidated by residence in Oxford, where he settled in 1654,
becoming a member of the group of Oxford thinkers known as the
'Invisible College' — which later formed the basis of the Royal
Society. His laboratory was a 'kind of Elysium', and in it he
carried out the experiments with the air-pump by which he
discovered the law of the pressure and volume of gases which
bears his name. A voluminous writer on a variety of scientific and
theological subjects, he was a modest man who consistently
refused the Presidency of the Royal Society, and was always
reluctant to be painted.

Opposite

120 HENRY PURCELL 1659-95
By Johann Baptist Closterman, 1695

This drawing is almost certainly Closterman's original *ad vivum*
study for his oil portrait of the composer, which is also in the
Gallery, and it has a freshness which is partly lost in the less
spontaneous painting. Certainly it is the closest we can get to
Purcell himself in the last year of his tragically short life. He was a
musical prodigy, and at the age of eight produced his first work, a
song, *Sweet Tyraness*. In 1669 he entered the Chapel Royal as a
choirboy, and received an intensive musical training, so that when
his voice broke he was equipped to follow a full-time career as a
professional musician. As composer in ordinary to Charles II and
organist of Westminster Abbey, he produced a stream of music for
church, theatre and court, often of great originality, and including
his masterpieces *Dido and Aeneas* and *The Faery Queen.*

123 WILLIAM III 1650-1702. Reigned 1688-1702
By an unknown artist after Sir Peter Lely, 1677

William, Stadholder of Holland, grandson of Charles I
and husband of Mary, the daughter of James II, had a
double reversionary claim to the throne of England. Thus
he was invited by a group of prominent Whigs to invade
England in 1688 in order to preserve Protestant liberties
which were threatened by the Roman Catholic James II.
James fled, and William and his wife Mary were jointly
given the throne, but on terms which banished for ever
the absolutism of the Tudors and Stuarts. As a lifelong
champion of European Protestantism, William formed the
Grand Alliance against France and the aggressive policies
of Louis XIV.

124 MARY II 1662-94. Reigned 1688-94
By an unknown artist adapted from William Wissing,
1685

The elder daughter of James II by Anne Hyde, Mary
married William of Orange in 1677, but they had no
children. In the heartbreaking dilemma of the Revolution
of 1688, Mary chose to support her husband and
Protestantism rather than her Catholic father. She came
to Whitehall 'laughing and jolly', and proved a wise and
tactful queen. In William's frequent absences she ruled
alone, but did not relish the experience. She died of
smallpox. In this elegant portrait she is shown as queen,
with the crown and sceptre by her and in robes of state,
surrounded by sweet-smelling flowers — roses and
honeysuckle.

Opposite
125 PRINCE JAMES FRANCIS EDWARD STUART (1688-1766), 'THE OLD PRETENDER', AND HIS SISTER PRINCESS LOUISA (1692-1712)
By Nicholas de Largillière, 1695

It was the birth of a male heir to the Catholic James II in
1688 which had precipitated the Revolution of that year;
Prince James was that heir, and he is shown in
Largillière's charming double portrait with all the
splendour of a future monarch, in a brilliant scarlet suit
which contrasts vividly with the blue Garter sash and his
sister's white dress. Whatever his claims, they were
doomed to disappointment. He was proclaimed king in
exile in France on the death of his father in 1701, but
despite a number of attempted landings in England, he
never came near the throne, and died in exile in Rome.

126 JOHN CHURCHILL, 1st DUKE OF MARLBOROUGH 1650-1722
By Sir Godfrey Kneller, c.1706

This brilliant oil sketch shows Queen Anne's great Commander-in-Chief, the victor of Blenheim and Ramillies, in triumph. On the left is Hercules with his club and a key (possibly a symbol of submission) and a woman offering a castle; under Marlborough's horse's hooves is the dishevelled figure of Discord, while in the clouds sits Justice; below her, Victory crowns the duke with laurel.

Below right
127 SARAH CHURCHILL, DUCHESS OF MARLBOROUGH 1660-1744
By an unknown artist after Sir Godfrey Kneller, c.1702

The beautiful Sarah Jennings became Lady-of-the-bedchamber to Princess, later Queen, Anne in 1683, and through the intimacy which developed she was able to further the military career of her husband, the duke.

Above
128 QUEEN ANNE (1665-1714; reigned 1702-14) AS PRINCESS OF DENMARK WITH HER SON WILLIAM, DUKE OF GLOUCESTER (1689-1700)
By an unknown artist after Sir Godfrey Kneller, c.1694

The second daughter of James II and his first wife Anne Hyde, Anne married Prince George of Denmark in 1683, and succeeded William III in 1702. For the whole of her reign this kind and generous woman was surrounded by warring political factions.
In her personal life she suffered greatly, losing all her many children in infancy. Prince William lived longer than the others, and by his death (aged eleven) opened up the Hanoverian succession.

Opposite
129 ROBERT HARLEY, 1st EARL OF OXFORD 1661-1724
By Sir Godfrey Kneller, 1714

It is ironical that Kneller's imposing full-length portrait of the Tory grandee in all the trappings of greatness — the Garter robes and his wand of office as Lord High Treasurer — catches him on the very brink of his fall from power. On her death-bed on 27 July 1714 Queen Anne finally dismissed the man who had overthrown Marlborough and Godolphin and sworn to end the French war. After the accession of George I, Harley was impeached on suspicion of Jacobitism. He was a shrewd intriguer, and a pioneer in the use of the political press. Pope and Swift were his apologists.

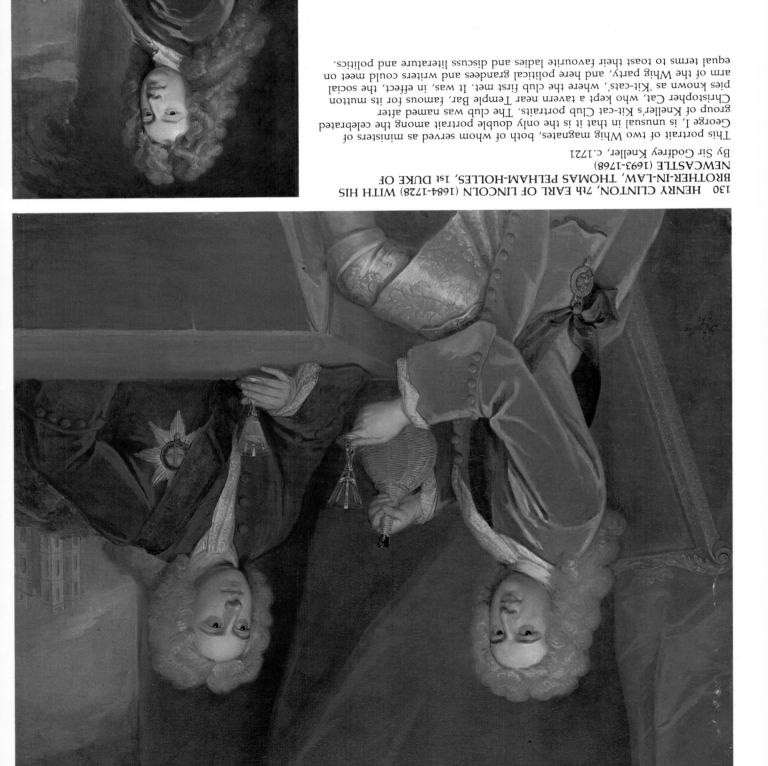

130 HENRY CLINTON, 7th EARL OF LINCOLN (1684-1728) WITH HIS BROTHER-IN-LAW, THOMAS PELHAM-HOLLES, 1st DUKE OF NEWCASTLE (1693-1768)
By Sir Godfrey Kneller, c.1721

This portrait of two Whig magnates, both of whom served as ministers of George I, is unusual in that it is the only double portrait among the celebrated group of Kneller's Kit-cat Club portraits. The club was named after Christopher Cat, who kept a tavern near Temple Bar, famous for its mutton pies known as 'Kit-cats', where the club first met. It was, in effect, the social arm of the Whig party, and here political grandees and writers could meet on equal terms to toast their favourite ladies and discuss literature and politics.

131 WILLIAM CONGREVE 1670-1729
By Sir Godfrey Kneller, 1709

Before he was thirty, Congreve had dazzled society with a succession of the wittiest comedies of manners ever written: *The Double Dealer, Love for Love,* and, above all, *The Way of the World.* Dryden considered him his natural successor, and his gifts made him a favourite at court, admired for his brilliant conversation. In this painting, another of Kneller's Kit-cat Club portraits (and an excellent example of the format, somewhere between a half-length and a threequarter-length, which he devised especially for them), he stresses Congreve's easy conversational manner. His urbane features are topped by a magnificent periwig which seems like a metaphor of the wearer's profusion of elegant wit.

Top row

132 Edward Hyde, 1st Earl of Clarendon 1609-74
After Adriaen Hanneman (detail)

133 Henrietta Anne, Duchess of Orleans 1644-70
After Pierre Mignard, c.1665-70

Second row

134 Barbara Palmer, Duchess of Cleveland 1640-1709
After Sir Peter Lely

135 Anthony Ashley-Cooper, 1st Earl of Shaftesbury 1621-83
After John Greenhill, c.1672-3

Third row

136 John Wilmot, 2nd Earl of Rochester 1647-80
After Jacob Huysmans, 1665-70

137 Sir William Temple 1628-99
Attributed to Sir Peter Lely, c.1660

138 Isaac Fuller 1606?-72
Self-portrait, c.1670

Fourth row

139 William III 1650-1702,
Reigned 1689-1702
By an unknown artist, 1690-1700

140 Grinling Gibbons 1648-1720
After Sir Godfrey Kneller, c.1690

141 Mary of Modena 1658-1718
By William Wissing, c.1685

142 John Locke 1632-1704
By Sylvester Brounower, 1685

Bottom row

143 William Bentinck, 1st Earl of Portland 1649-1709
Studio of Hyacinthe Rigaud, 1698-9

144 Henry St John, Viscount Bolingbroke 1678-1751
Attributed to Alexis Simeon Belle

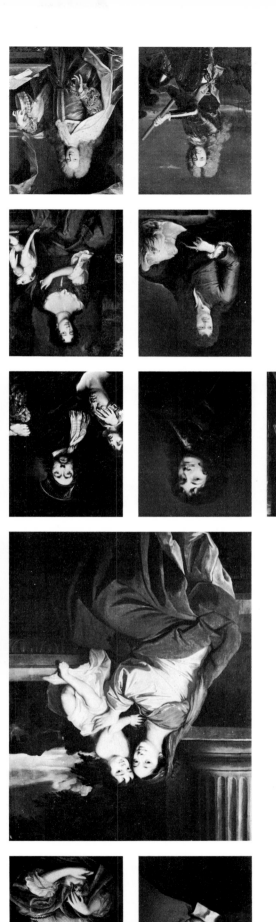

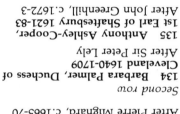

GEORGIAN BRITAIN

The eighteenth century was a period of political and social stability; radicalism, the mob and the collapse of the *ancien régime* in France were doubly feared because memories of the troubles of the seventeenth century were all too vivid. The first two Georges were accepted because they had no policies, and England was effectively governed by a rich, largely Whig, aristocracy, whose great country houses, built and furnished by such architects as Kent and Adam, and filled with pictures and statues acquired on the Grand Tour, were the embodiment of their territorial power. It was an age of increasing national wealth, of expansion overseas, of fortunes made in the West Indies and later in India; and of retribution in America. It was the age of the industrial revolution: of inventions like Watt's steam-engine, far-reaching technological change and improvements in communications, the growth of large-scale enterprise and the factory system, and the spread of banking. But the expectation of life remained low — disease struck indiscriminately at all classes — and progress entailed declining independence and conditions of work for the poorer members of the community. In 1714 the population was five and a half million; by the census of 1801 it had reached nine million. In 1714 England was largely rural, and only one town was of any size, London with its population of half a million; by 1790 the depopulation of the countryside, as a result of enclosures and economic farming, had begun in earnest, and of the new industrial towns of the north, Manchester was approaching a population of 150,000. Cast iron, the mills, the canals, the turnpike roads and the stage coach had changed the face of England.

As in the seventeenth century, the court remained the centre of political, social and, to some extent, artistic life. Queen Caroline patronized Handel, George III, Zoffany and West. Opposition courts were even more influential on the arts. Frederick, Prince of Wales, actively encouraged the artists of the rococo; the Prince Regent, patron of Gainsborough, intended Carlton House to be enriched with royal portraits. Both loved painting as only Charles I had. Portraiture remained the staple of the British artist; much continued to be done by itinerant or provincial artists, the most distinguished of whom was Joseph Wright of Derby, who painted Arkwright and other inventors and industrial entrepreneurs. Successive attempts to improve the status of the British artist resulted, in 1768, in the foundation of the Royal Academy, of which Joshua (later Sir Joshua) Reynolds became the first President. Reynolds was determined that British art should emulate the academic ideals of Raphael and Poussin and the Bolognese painters of the seventeenth century, and his own work gained a calculated nobility from its borrowed compositions and poses. But eighteenth-century life also had its squalid side, and appalling wretchedness and poverty, upon which, paradoxically, the fine craftsmanship of the century depended, lay behind the success of salvationists such as Wesley. It was Hogarth who portrayed the London poor, and Hogarth who represented the new middle class who read the *Tatler* and *Spectator*, went to Lillo's plays and *The Beggar's Opera*, and created the market for cheap engravings. Later-eighteenth-century reproductive art encompassed, on the one hand, the portrait mezzotints which were the chief glory of British print-making, and, on the other, the caricatures of Rowlandson and Gillray. They are as representative of the age as the grand full-lengths of Gainsborough or Reynolds.

145   GEORGE II 1683-1760. Reigned 1727-60
By Thomas Hudson, 1744

George II was the last British sovereign to command in the field, and his personal gallantry at the Battle of Dettingen (1743) made him a popular hero overnight. Vacillating in political crises, his interests lay in the pomp and ceremonial of royalty, and his favourite study was the genealogy of the German princely families. This image of the small and dapper king has something of the swagger and vitality of French royal portraiture of the rococo.

146 FREDERICK, PRINCE OF WALES (1707-51) AND HIS SISTERS
By Philip Mercier, 1733

Both the first two Georges hated their eldest sons. Frederick set up a lively opposition court at Leicester House, and Bolingbroke, Chesterfield and the young 'Patriots' who opposed Walpole were among his special friends; while George II patronized Handel, Frederick supported the rival Italian opera. He was a genuine lover of painting and encouraged the avant-garde artists of the rococo, of whom Mercier was one. In this conversation piece Frederick is seen playing the 'cello, and two of his sisters the harpsichord and a form of lute, while the third has a volume of Milton open in her lap; in the background is the Dutch House at Kew.

147 PRINCE CHARLES EDWARD STUART 1720-88
Studio of Antonio David, c.1729?

The Jacobite cause, centred on the court at St Germain near Paris, was revitalized by 'Bonnie Prince Charlie', the Young Pretender. Securing the promise of French military support (which never materialized), the prince set sail for Scotland in 1745. Through the sheer attraction of his own personality he found an enthusiastic following, occupied Edinburgh, won a victory at Prestonpans, continued to outwit the English generals, and terrified the Government by reaching Derby. There the resolution of his staff failed to match his own, and a demoralizing retreat ended with the slaughter of Culloden. After a romantic escape, the prince returned to France, from which he was banished in 1748, and subsequently led a wandering life, a victim of drunken habits.

148   QUEEN CAROLINE 1683-1737
By Jacopo Amigoni, 1735

Queen Caroline possessed a deep sympathy for science, literature and
the arts, encouraged by her youthful sojourn at the court of the
intellectual Queen of Prussia, friend of Leibnitz. She busied herself with
the gardens at Kensington Palace — one of the first English landscape
gardens — and it was she who discovered, in a bureau drawer, the
magnificent Holbein drawings now at Windsor. She was the friend of
Newton, Halley and Pope, and an ardent supporter of Handel. In
politics she had a stronger will than her husband, George II, and her
support of Walpole was unwavering.

149 SIR ROBERT WALPOLE, 1st EARL OF ORFORD 1676-1745
Studio of Jean Baptiste van Loo, c.1740

Sir Robert Walpole, who came to power through his management of the South Sea Bubble crisis, laid the foundations for the unparalleled prosperity of the eighteenth century. Through sheer hard work and administrative skill, an uncanny understanding of human motives and the calculated use of patronage ('every man has his price'), Walpole virtually created, by his own abilities, the office of Prime Minister. His policies were devoted to the encouragement of trade and investment through the reduction of taxation and the national debt, and he was determined to avoid an aggressive foreign policy. When war with Spain was forced on him in 1739 he said bitterly to the Duke of Newcastle: 'It is your war and I wish you joy of it'. His power sapped by the opposition court of Frederick, Prince of Wales, and by the death of his staunch ally, Queen Caroline, he was driven out of office in 1742. In private life he loved field sports, built one of the most beautiful of Palladian houses, Houghton, and amassed a magnificent collection of pictures, later sold *en bloc* to Catherine of Russia.

150 GEORGE FREDERICK HANDEL 1685-1759
By Thomas Hudson, 1756

Handel, then Kapellmeister to the Elector of Hanover (later George I), first visited London in 1710-11 and achieved an immediate triumph with his opera, *Rinaldo*, sumptuously produced at the Queen's Theatre, Haymarket. His celebrated *Water Music* was composed for a royal journey by barge from Whitehall to Limehouse. At the accession of George II and Queen Caroline, his principal patrons, he became court composer and was naturalized. From the mid-1730s he devoted his energies to the great oratorios which have sustained the English choral tradition to this day: *Saul* was first performed in 1739, and *Messiah* in 1742. It was his friend, Charles Jennens, librettist of both, who commissioned the portrait by Hudson. A 'state portrait' of a middle-class sitter — Handel is shown wearing a sword and with his hand tucked into his waistcoat in the manner approved by the etiquette books — the picture shows Handel's familiar bushy eyebrows and sour expression.

**151 WILLS HILL,
1st MARQUESS OF DOWNSHIRE
(1718-93) AND HIS FAMILY**
By Arthur Devis, c.1760
(On loan from the Marchioness of
Downshire Discretionary Trust)

The conversation piece, in which
Devis specialized, was first
popularized in the mid-1720s by
Philip Mercier (see plate 146) and
developed by Hogarth. Devis's
pictures, with their beautifully
painted detail, especially the costume,
have a naive charm; his rather doll-
like figures are often linked by
gestures and suggest the pleasures of
domesticity as well as the possession
of broad acres.

**152 RICHARD BOYLE, 3rd EARL
OF BURLINGTON 1694-1753**
Attributed to Jonathan Richardson,
c.1717-19

Horace Walpole called Burlington the
'Apollo of arts'. Inspired by his
travels in Italy, he became an
amateur architect and one of the
founders of the Palladian movement.
His finest surviving achievements are
the Assembly Rooms, York (a replica
of the Egyptian Hall described by
Vitruvius), and his own villa at
Chiswick, derived from Palladio's
Villa Rotunda. In this portrait
Burlington holds a pair of dividers,
and the bagnio (bath-house) at
Chiswick is seen in the background.

154 LADY MARY WORTLEY MONTAGU (1689-1762) WITH HER SON EDWARD
Attributed to Jean Baptiste Vanmour, c.1717

Lady Mary Wortley Montagu was a leader in early Georgian society, best known for her famous *Letters*. She accompanied her husband on his embassy to Constantinople (seen in the background of this portrait, where she is depicted in Turkish dress), observed the practice of inoculation for smallpox, which she introduced into England, and spent the last twenty years of her life abroad.

Right
155 SAMUEL RICHARDSON 1689-1761
By Joseph Highmore, 1750

Richardson set up as a printer in 1719, first in Fleet Street and then in Salisbury Court. A modest, virtuous man of nervous disposition, his sentimental novels *Pamela* and *Clarissa Harlowe* exactly suited the middle-class ethic of his day. Among his enthusiastic correspondents was Lady Bradshaigh, depicted here with her husband and their home, Haigh Hall, in the picture by Devis seen over the mantelpiece.

Opposite
153 JONATHAN SWIFT 1667-1745
By Charles Jervas, c.1718

Swift became a political pamphleteer in the Tory cause, despite his friendship with the Whig writers and wits, Addison, Steele and Congreve. His hopes of patronage destroyed in 1714, he became increasingly misanthropic, and died insane. Even from his early *Tale of a Tub* and *Battle of the Books* his satires were spiced with scorn and malice. His best-known book is *Gulliver's Travels* (1726).

156   A CONVERSATION OF VIRTUOSIS... AT THE KINGS ARMES
By Gawen Hamilton, 1735

This picture was seen in 1734 by the celebrated antiquary George Vertue: 'a Conversation of Virtuosis that usually meet at the Kings Arms. New bond Street a noted tavern. is truely a Master piece as far as is done'. Vertue is seen on the extreme left; Gibbs, the architect, is holding a scroll of paper; rather resplendent, fourth from the right, is Wootton, the sporting painter, resting his hand on the shoulder of Rysbrack, the sculptor; the next figure is a self-portrait, and on the right is Burlington's protégé, William Kent. The group is a close imitation of Hogarth.

157   WILLIAM HOGARTH 1697-1764
Self-portrait, c.1757

Hogarth, the chief exponent of the rococo style in England, was a crusader for British art. Who else would have signed himself: W. Hogarth *Anglus*? He started the St Martin's Lane Academy, found employment for his fellow artists at the Foundling Hospital and Vauxhall Gardens, and wrote a treatise on painting, *The Analysis of Beauty*. His 'modern moral subjects', such as *The Rake's Progress* and *Marriage à la Mode*, were highly original, and he was the first English artist to popularize his works through engraving. This self-portrait amply demonstrates his determination and pugnacity.

158   FRANCIS HAYMAN 1708-76
Self-portrait

Hayman was as versatile an artist as his friend Hogarth. He worked with the French draughtsman Gravelot (the teacher of Gainsborough) on illustrated books, and was a scene painter at Drury Lane Theatre. He helped to popularize the conversation piece with landscape setting (later to be transformed by Gainsborough) and, with his assistants, was responsible for the series of large decorative canvases which adorned the supper boxes at Vauxhall Gardens, the most spectacular place of outdoor evening entertainment in London. He was an active promoter of the Society of Artists, an exhibiting body of which he was President from 1766 to 1768, when he seceded to the new Royal Academy, where he was Librarian from 1771. The seated figure has not been identified.

159   HORACE WALPOLE, 4th EARL OF ORFORD 1717-97
By John Giles Eccardt, 1754

Horace Walpole, fourth son of the Prime Minister, was one of the most graceful and amusing men of of his age, welcomed by every hostess. His celebrated letters, written to a host of friends, including the poet, Thomas Gray, with whom he went on the Grand Tour, are full of gossip, anecdote and description expressed with incomparable style and wit. He hated Houghton, his father's Norfolk home, and all country pursuits, but he catalogued the famous picture collection there. In 1747 he bought his own estate at Twickenham, which he named Strawberry Hill; the conversion of the house into a Gothic castle, seen in the background of Eccardt's portrait, and its furnishing with works of art and curiosities of all kinds, became his life's work.

71

160 THE DEATH OF WILLIAM PITT, 1st EARL OF CHATHAM 1708-78
By John Singleton Copley, 1779-81
(On loan from the Tate Gallery)

Pitt was in every respect the opposite of Walpole. His father was a volatile East Indian adventurer nicknamed 'Diamond' Pitt; he was a manic-depressive frequently unable to cope with business; he had little understanding of either men or politics. A fervent believer in liberty and free speech, an orator who carried passionate conviction and one of the greatest statesmen in British history, his deep concern was the French threat to our overseas trade. Grudgingly given high office a year after the outbreak of the Seven Years War, he chose brilliant commanders and led the country to glorious victories throughout the world. Always known as the 'Great Commoner', though he accepted an earldom, he is depicted by Copley collapsing in the House of Lords after speaking in support of the rights of the American colonists.

161 GEORGE III 1738-1820. Reigned 1760-1820
Studio of Allan Ramsay, c.1767

George III ascended the throne determined to break the rule of the powerful Whig families and to restore something of the lost power of the crown. In this he was ultimately thwarted. The firmness of his views, often amounting to obstinacy, brought disaster to the country when he refused to recognize the legitimate grievances of the American colonists ('No taxation without representation'). Industrious and painstaking, George III was especially interested in farming, mechanics and books: his collection forms the nucleus of the King's Library in the British Museum. He founded the Royal Academy, but favoured West rather than Reynolds. As he became subject to more and more serious fits of insanity (due to porphyria), Parliament was obliged, in 1811, to pass a Regency Bill, and his last ten years were spent incapacitated by illness and blindness.

162   JOHN STUART, 3rd EARL OF BUTE 1713-92
By Sir Joshua Reynolds, 1773

Bute was the constant companion of the young prince later to become
George III, and instilled in him Bolingbroke's theory that a king should
not only reign but govern. An incompetent and irresolute Prime
Minister, who made an unpopular peace with the French in 1763, he was
vilified and lampooned as a royal favourite and a Scot. Reynolds's
grand full-length, based on the pose of the Apollo Belvedere, is an
excellent portrait of the handsome, proud and pompous courtier.

163 DOCTOR SAMUEL JOHNSON 1709-84
By Sir Joshua Reynolds, 1756

Reynolds's portrait shows Johnson with his recently completed *Dictionary*, a work of prodigious effort. Massive, ungainly, plagued with nervous tics, he was a victim of melancholia and could not bear solitude. He had an immense circle of friends, and was one of the greatest conversationalists of all time. Though an authoritarian churchman and high Tory, overbearing and full of prejudice, yet tenderness and humanitarianism were dominant features of his character.

164 FRANCES D'ARBLAY (FANNY BURNEY) 1752-1840
By Edward Francis Burney (her cousin)

The daughter of Dr Charles Burney, musician and author of *The History of Music*, Fanny Burney began writing stories at the age of ten, and her first novel, *Evelina*, later admired by Jane Austen, was published anonymously in 1778. For some years employed at court, in 1793 she married a refugee from the French Revolution, General d'Arblay. She is now best known for her vividly descriptive *Diary*.

165 JAMES BOSWELL 1740-95
By Sir Joshua Reynolds, 1785

Boswell was a Scottish country gentleman with a passion for the pleasures and fashionable life of London. His famous meeting with Johnson took place in 1763 in Davies's bookshop in Covent Garden. Boswell set himself to record Johnson's conversation verbatim, and to elicit his views on every conceivable topic, and the merit of the great *Life* lies in its dialogue. Through Boswell, many of the Doctor's pungent aphorisms have passed into the language.

167   CARL FRIEDRICH ABEL 1725-87
By Thomas Gainsborough, c.1762-5

Abel was the last great virtuoso player of the viola da gamba, which, though it was already obsolescent, he regarded as 'the king of instruments'. With J.C. Bach, with whom he shared a house from 1762 till 1773, he organized what were to become one of the most celebrated features of eighteenth-century London musical life, the subscription concerts chiefly associated with the Hanover Square Rooms. He was also a member of Queen Charlotte's private orchestra. A great admirer of the fine arts, he was an intimate friend and boon companion of Gainsborough, many of whose drawings he owned, and who had loved him 'from the moment I heard him touch the string'.

166   LAURENCE STERNE 1713-68
By Sir Joshua Reynolds, 1760

Reynolds's classically composed portrait, incorporating the familiar gesture of the hand held to the forehead, traditional in portraits of authors and philosophers, represents Sterne at the moment of his greatest success, when *Tristram Shandy* was the talk of the town. Sterne's digressiveness, inconsequential style and indecency in expression were a novelty in eighteenth-century literature; Richardson called the book 'execrable', and Johnson always spoke of Sterne with scorn. Akin to Rousseau in his sensibility and lack of self-control, Sterne's *Sentimental Journey* made an instant appeal to French taste.

168 SIR JOSHUA REYNOLDS (1723-92), SIR WILLIAM CHAMBERS (1726-96) AND JOSEPH WILTON (1722-1803)
By John Francis Rigaud, 1782

Reynolds, Chambers and Wilton — respectively painter, architect and sculptor — were all founder members of the Royal Academy, established in 1768. Reynolds, close friend of Johnson, Burke and Goldsmith, and a sensitive host, was the first President, and set the high academic tone of the new institution not only by his own classicizing style but through his celebrated annual Discourses. Chambers, the first Treasurer, architect of Somerset House, had the ear of the king, who was unfavourably disposed towards Reynolds, and was in some ways a malicious rival of the president. Wilton, lifelong friend of Chambers, became Keeper in 1790.

169 THOMAS GAINSBOROUGH 1727-88
Self-portrait, c.1759

Gainsborough was a professional portrait painter whose chief love was landscape. ('If the People with their damn'd Faces could but let me alone a little...') Yet, in contrast to Reynolds and most of his contemporaries, he customarily executed both costume and setting with his own hand, and the sheer beauty of his handling of paint is unequalled in British art. He regarded likeness as 'the principal beauty and intention of a portrait', but his landscapes were imaginary, and expressed a nostalgic view of country life. He was the opposite of intellectual, many of his friends were musicians, and his letters have the brilliance and idiosyncrasy of Sterne.

170　GEORGE STUBBS 1724-1806
Self-portrait, 1781

Stubbs had no interest in the Grand Manner
or in classical antiquity, and travelled to Rome
with the aim of reassuring himself that nature
was superior to art. He is best known for his
Anatomy of the Horse, a series of magnificent
engravings based on the dissections he carried
out in a remote village in Lincolnshire. Stubbs
was a superb animal painter and a penetrating
portraitist, notably of working people he
esteemed, such as stable-lads. His *Mares and
Foals* compositions are unequalled for
rhythmic elegance, while his *Lion and Horse*
paintings foreshadow the wild and dramatic
subject-matter of romanticism.

171　ALLAN RAMSAY 1713-84
Self-portrait, c.1739

Ramsay was trained in Rome and Naples, and this early self-
portrait shows his indebtedness to the vigour of the Italian
baroque. On his return to London, he wrote: 'I have put all your
Vanlois and Soldis and Ruscas to flight and now play the first
fiddle myself'. His only serious competitor was Hudson (see plate
(150), with whom he shared a drapery painter, Van Aken, and it
was he, not Reynolds, who was appointed Principal Painter to the
King in 1761. Ramsay's portraits are characterized by their soft
colours and French elegance.

172   ROBERT, 1st LORD CLIVE 1725-74
Studio of Nathaniel Dance

Clive was the son of an impoverished country squire, and went out
to Madras as an East India Company clerk at the age of eighteen.
Turning to a military career, he won renown for his daring and
established his reputation by the heroic defence of Arcot. During the
Seven Years War he extended British influence through his
manipulation of the native rulers and, after the relief of Calcutta and
the victory of Plassey in 1757, was virtually the ruler of Bengal.
Following a period as Governor of Bengal, Clive was forced by ill-
health to leave India for the last time. Though he had undoubtedly
made a fortune in the East, the denunciation of his rule by which he
was hounded on his return was both malicious and grossly unfair,
and at the Parliamentary enquiry he declared: 'By God, Mr.
Chairman, at this moment I stand astonished at my own
moderation!' Subject to fits of depression, he committed suicide at the
age of forty-nine.

173   CAPTAIN JAMES COOK 1728-79
By John Webber, 1776

Cook led three expeditions to the Pacific at the instance of the
Royal Society, spending over eight years at sea. On the first
expedition, in which he lost a third of his men, he charted New
Zealand and the east coast of Australia; Botany Bay still retains
the name given to it by Cook's naturalists, who included
Joseph (later Sir Joseph) Banks. The object of the second
expedition was to explore the myth of a great southern
continent, and was memorable for the elimination of scurvy
and fever. On the third expedition, in search of a passage
round the north of America, on which the draughtsman was
John Webber, the artist of this portrait, Cook was clubbed to
death in the Sandwich Islands.

174 WARREN HASTINGS 1732-1818
By Sir Joshua Reynolds, 1766-8

As Governor of Bengal, Hastings engaged in far-reaching judicial and administrative reforms and as the first Governor-General he successfully consolidated the empire established by Clive. No administrator in the complex political situation that prevailed could hope to govern without some degree of irregularity, and, largely through the vehement priggishness of Burke, Hastings was impeached for corruption on his return to England. Though finally acquitted, the trial dragged on for seven years and cost Hastings seventy thousand pounds. Reynolds's portrait, showing the young Hastings, before he was broken in health by his ordeal, is one of his noblest compositions.

175 JOHN JERVIS, EARL OF ST VINCENT 1735-1823
By Francis Cotes, 1769

As Commander-in-Chief in the Mediterranean, Jervis's injection of harsh measures into the discipline of the Fleet made his name a byword among officers and men alike. However, the efficiency of the Fleet improved to such a pitch as a result of his methods that at the Battle of Cape St Vincent, on St Valentine's Day 1797, with fifteen ships of the line lying in wait for the Spanish Fleet of twenty-seven, he inflicted so crushing a defeat on the enemy that England was relieved of the very real threat of invasion by Napoleon's armies. Jervis was awarded an earldom, proposing Yarmouth or Orford in order to avoid a charge of arrogance, but the king himself insisted on the title of St Vincent so that a glorious victory should live on in his name.

176 ADMIRAL HORATIO NELSON, VISCOUNT NELSON 1758-1805
By Guy Head, 1798

Nelson achieved a similar discipline and efficiency as did St Vincent, but by different means — a form of charisma inspiring an influence described by contemporaries as admiration, respect, devotion and even love. His three victories — the Nile, Copenhagen and Trafalgar — were vital in stemming the tide of the Napoleonic advance through Europe, earning him his place as an international hero and the title 'the Immortal Nelson'. Guy Head's romantic idealization shows Nelson receiving the French Admiral's sword after the Battle of the Nile. The sword in fact was presented to him by the *Vanguard*'s First Lieutenant and not by a midshipman, and Nelson himself was desperately wounded, his head bound with a bloodstained bandage. The scene at midnight on the quarterdeck would have been very different.

Opposite
177 ADMIRAL HORATIO NELSON, VISCOUNT NELSON 1758-1805
By Sir William Beechey, 1800-1

Beechey's vivid sketch is a study for the whole-length portrait commissioned by the City of Norwich and painted between Nelson's landing at Yarmouth in November 1800 and the victory of Copenhagen in April 1801. It cost the Chamberlain of Norwich two hundred guineas. The sketch shows the artist's alteration to the shape of the head and the hideous wound inflicted over Nelson's right eye at the Nile; curiously, the colour of his eyes is painted brown instead of grey. On the back is the inscription *WB pinx! Presented to his beloved son Captn Beechey 1830*. It descended through the Beechey family until sold in London in 1966, bought by Mr Hugh Leggatt and placed on loan to the Gallery by the Trustees of Mr Hugh Leggatt's Settlement.

179 FITZROY SOMERSET, 1st LORD RAGLAN 1788-1855
By Thomas Heaphy, 1813-14

As Lord Fitzroy Somerset, eighth son of the Duke of Beaufort, he served in the Peninsula as Wellington's ADC, at Waterloo where he lost an arm ('take care of my rings' he said as it fell to the ground), on several diplomatic missions, and as ADC to George IV. He was appointed Field-Marshal and Commander-in-Chief in the Crimean War, was victorious at Alma and Inkerman, and died in the camp before Sebastopol.

178 MAJOR-GENERAL SIR EDWARD PAKENHAM 1778-1815
By Thomas Heaphy, 1813-14

Pakenham served with Wellington in the Peninsula, especially distinguishing himself at Salamanca, 'the best-manoeuvred battle in the whole war'. He was awarded clasps for nine campaigns and was killed in America in the unsuccessful assault on General Jackson's army before New Orleans. His sister Catherine married the Duke of Wellington.

182 WILLIAM CARR, VISCOUNT BERESFORD 1768-1854
By Thomas Heaphy, 1813-14

Beresford was an illegitimate son of the Marquess of Waterford. He served with distinction with Baird in Egypt, and with Moore in the Peninsula, and his achievement in reorganizing the Portuguese army earned him the rank of Marshal-General. 'A low-looking ruffian with damned bad manners', said Creevey; 'the ablest man in the army', said Wellington.

181 ROWLAND HILL, 1st VISCOUNT HILL 1772-1842
By Thomas Heaphy, 1813-14

Hill served at Aboukir in 1801, in the Peninsula where he distinguished himself at the bloody storming of Almarez, and finally at Waterloo, where his brigade engaged the Imperial Guard at close quarters, his horse being killed under him. Lord Hill's column, erected near Shrewsbury, his home town, bears the roll of eighteen victories. 'A dependable officer', said Wellington; 'a very dull man', said Melbourne.

Centre

180 ARTHUR WELLESLEY, 1st DUKE OF WELLINGTON 1769-1852
By Thomas Heaphy, 1813-14

The legendary hero, 'the Iron Duke', did more than any man to lead Europe to victory in the long-drawn-out struggle against Napoleon, culminating at Waterloo in 1815. Later the weight of his immense prestige led him into politics, and he was twice prime minister, though less successfully. He became Queen Victoria and Prince Albert's trusted friend and adviser, and was godfather to their third son, Prince Arthur; and when the queen asked him how to solve the problem of birds fouling the exhibits in the Crystal Palace he replied 'try sparrow-hawks, Ma'am!'. Heaphy painted his collection of portraits of Peninsular veterans after the Battle of Vitoria in 1813.

Top row

**183   George I 1660-1727.
Reigned 1714-27**
By Michael Rysbrack, c.1732

184   Edward Gibbon 1737-94
By Henry Walton, 1773

Second row

185   Sir Hans Sloane 1660-1753
By Stephen Slaughter, 1736

186   Alexander Pope 1688-1744
By William Hoare, c.1739?

187   John Wesley 1703-91
By Nathaniel Hone, 1766

188   David Garrick 1717-79
By Thomas Gainsborough, c.1770

Third row

189   Robert Adam 1728-92
By an unknown artist

**190   Thomas Augustine Arne
1710-78**
After Francesco Bartolozzi

191   William Cowper 1731-1800
By George Romney, 1792

192   Robert Burns 1759-96
By Alexander Nasmyth

Fourth row

193   William Pitt 1759-1806
By John Hoppner

194   Charles James Fox 1749-1806
By Karl Anton Hickel

195   Sarah Siddons 1755-1831
By John Downman, 1787

Bottom row

**196   Emma, Lady Hamilton
1761?-1815**
By George Romney, c.1785

**197   Richard Brinsley Sheridan
1751-1816**
By John Russell, 1788

THE REGENCY

The word 'Regency' immediately conjures up a vision of debauchery, gambling, heavy eating and drinking, mistresses, a flashy style of portraiture, a flamboyant if not downright vulgar architecture and décor, and in fact an eponymous age reflecting the life-style of the Prince Regent himself. The gossip-writers of the day, satirists like Gillray and Cruikshank, and a host of novelettes from that day to this, have seen to it that the legend persists.

The legend, it must be faced, does contain several degrees of truth. In many ways George was a thoroughly unattractive man, his way of life colouring a period sandwiched between Augustan elegance and Victorian sobriety. His behaviour on occasions, and not only to his wife, could be monstrous. He deserted his Whig friends in an hour of crisis; he was unforgiving to Beau Brummel; and he ate and drank copiously, though even Creevey 'never saw him the least drunk but once'.

But there is another distinct side to the coin. George was a patron and connoisseur of some flair. He added distinction to the Royal Collection, especially in the field of portraiture. He presented his father's library to the British Museum, which itself owes much to his encouragement; he urged the Government to buy the Angerstein collection, thus forming the nucleus of the National Gallery; he sent £200 to Beethoven; Jane Austen herself dedicated *Emma* to him with words reflecting the opinion of most of his subjects, and ending 'His Royal Highness's Dutiful and Obedient Humble Servant'.

In simplified terms the period is a watershed between eighteenth-century complacency and the age of industrial and social reform. Although the Regency itself only existed formally between 1811 and 1820, when the Prince of Wales acted legally as Regent for his insane father, the word is generally recognized to cover the first quarter of the century. England struggled, often alone, against the tyranny of Napoleon, and peaks like Cape St Vincent, Trafalgar and Waterloo epitomize a long-drawn-out conflict maintained at first by professional sailors and soldiers but shared eventually by the whole nation. Against this background Prinny's excesses melt into insignificance.

Accompanying the wars, another sort of revolution was taking place. Industry was benefiting from the effects of Watt's steam-engine, Arkwright's spinning-jenny and the inventions of McAdam and Brunel. The evils of slavery, convict ships, child labour and a Draconic penal system, were being met by the reforming zeal of Wilberforce, Clarkson, Elizabeth Fry, Burdett, Francis Place, John Howard and many others. Cobbett's *Rural Rides* (1830) provide a vivid account of Regency England, its farming, rural industries, country houses, rotten boroughs, and the gradual emergence of a large proportion of Englishmen from misery and starvation.

Parallel with these great trends ran the Romantic Movement — broadly speaking a European reaction to the sterility of classical inhibition. The giants were Beethoven, Voltaire, Rousseau, Goya and Delacroix, but the British contribution was no less formidable. Wordsworth, Coleridge and Shelley opened men's eyes to a new life. 'Bliss was it in that dawn to be alive, But to be young was very heaven!' The works of Scott, Byron's *Don Juan*, the lyrics of Keats and Blake, all added a new depth to a period of unrest and growing excitement. The visions of Beethoven and Turner are timeless and transcendental but they are part of the Romantic Movement and as such belong to the Regency.

198   GEORGE IV 1762-1830. Regent 1811-20; reigned 1820-30
By Sir Thomas Lawrence, 1814

Lawrence was presented to the Prince Regent in 1814, and granted four or five sittings, the prince coming to his studio for the purpose. This oil sketch, which also relates very closely to a drawing in the Royal Library, is possibly one of the original studies for the innumerable glamorized portraits of George, both as regent and as king, with which Lawrence has immortalized his face and figure. The theory that it was also used for the coinage is probably unfounded.

199 CAROLINE OF BRUNSWICK, QUEEN OF GEORGE IV 1768-1821
By Sir Thomas Lawrence, 1804

Caroline married the Prince of Wales in 1795 but her appearance and behaviour revolted him and they separated a year later. Their only child, Princess Charlotte, was a source of constant friction between them, eventually causing Princess Caroline to indulge in a round of scandalous eccentricity leading to the so-called 'trial' in the House of Lords and her exclusion from the coronation ceremony in Westminster Abbey. Lawrence's portrait shows her with a bust of her father, the Duke of Brunswick, and in her hand a modelling tool indicating her skill as a sculptor.

200 CHARLOTTE AUGUSTA, PRINCESS OF WALES 1796-1817
By George Dawe, 1817

Charlotte was daughter of the Prince Regent and Princess Caroline; she married Leopold of Belgium and died in childbirth a year later. Their son would have been heir to the throne. According to the Tsar's sister, Catherine, she was 'white, fresh and appetising as possible with large light blue lively eyes which on occasion get the fixed stare of the House of Brunswick'.

201 MARIA FITZHERBERT 1756-1837
By Sir Joshua Reynolds, c.1788
(On loan from the Earl of Portarlington)

Mrs Fitzherbert, a Roman Catholic and twice widowed, married the Prince of Wales in her own drawing-room at Richmond. The marriage, never publicly acknowledged, contravened the 1772 Act precluding the royal family from marrying without the king's consent, but George treated her as his wife and they were happy together until he was forced into the farcical union with Princess Caroline.

202 THE TRIAL OF QUEEN CAROLINE 1820
By Sir George Hayter, 1823

After her disastrous marriage to the Prince Regent, and
partly as a result of his unkindness and lack of sympathy,
Princess Caroline gave way to a life of flagrant debauchery
ranging throughout Europe. This caused a series of semi-
official investigations leading finally to divorce proceedings
when, at the death of George III, she returned to England
in 1820. The 'trial' in the House of Lords took the shape of
a debate on a Bill of Pains and Penalties. It was marked by
the eloquence of her defending counsel, Lord Brougham,
the ludicrous behaviour of the witnesses, especially
Majocci whose repetition of 'non mi ricordi' became a
popular refrain, and finally the adjournment of the
proceedings by the Prime Minister, Lord Liverpool. On the
whole, public feeling supported Caroline, but she was
repulsed from George's coronation at the doors of
Westminster Abbey and died a fortnight later.

A VOLUPTUARY under the horrors of Digestion.

203 A VOLUPTUARY under the horrors of Digestion
By James Gillray, 1792

The dissipations of the prince were notorious but
exaggerated, and caricaturists like Gillray and Cruikshank
insulting and merciless. Here he is shown with fork to
mouth and bursting belly amid the ruins of a meal and
decanters of port and brandy; a brimming chamber-pot
stands on a commode, together with unpaid bills. Other
unsavoury allusions to the prince's life-style adorn the
background. Above his head is Tintoretto's portrait of
Luigi Cornaro, author of *Discorri della vita sobria*, who
changed a life of youthful excess to one of rigorous
asceticism and lived to the age of ninety-nine. The prince
appears oblivious of the sarcasm.

204 SIR WALTER SCOTT 1771-1832
By Sir Edwin Landseer, 1824

The poetry and novels of Scott are full of a
unique compound of racy narrative, Scottish
legend and history, antiquarian lore and a
profound insight into human nature. *The Lay of
the Last Minstrel* (1805) met with instant and
resounding success, followed by *Marmion* and
then the *Waverley Novels* — a prodigious
output of at least one novel a year, representing
the flower of the Romantic Movement.
Landseer's portrait, painted at Abbotsford,
shows Scott at the height of his powers, two
years before the financial crash which darkened
the remaining years of his life.

205 WILLIAM WORDSWORTH 1770-1850
By Benjamin Haydon, 1818

Wordsworth's poetry, a main-spring in the
Romantic Movement, is imbued with nature in
every mood from the sublime to the serene.
Haydon's drawing shows divine inspiration
fading and Wordsworth listening to 'the still,
sad music of humanity'.

206 SAMUEL TAYLOR COLERIDGE 1772-1834
By Peter Vandyke, 1795

The portrait shows Coleridge, author of *Kubla
Khan, The Ancient Mariner*, and, with
Wordsworth, *The Lyrical Ballads*, engaged in the
inspired monologue which both delighted and
exasperated his friends.

207 GEORGE GORDON, LORD BYRON 1788-1824
By Thomas Phillips, 1813

Byron's wild life-style and sombre poems have become symbolic of the Romantic Movement, haunting the imagination of Europe. The first cantos of *Childe Harold* emerged in 1812 and made him famous overnight at the age of twenty-four. Of *Don Juan* (1819-23) Shelley said 'every word has the stamp of immortality'. Phillips's portrait shows the poet as one of the young lords of creation, arrayed in the Arnaout costume he bought in Epirus in 1809. The costume itself is now in the Assembly Rooms in Bath. Byron's letters are among the masterpieces of that elusive art.

208 JOHN KEATS 1795-1821
By Joseph Severn, 1819

Keats's most magical poety — *The Eve of St Agnes, The Grecian Urn, A Nightingale* and *La Belle Dame sans Merci* — was written in under two years, before his untimely death in Rome.

209 PERCY BYSSHE SHELLEY 1792-1822
By Amelia Curran, 1819

Shelley's inspired affirmation of the values of art was proclaimed in the essay *A Defence of Poetry*, and in the poems *Prometheus Unbound, Ode to the West Wind*, and *To a Skylark*.

210 JOHN CONSTABLE 1776-1837
By Ramsay Richard Reinagle, c.1799

Constable's landscape paintings, mostly of East Anglia, Wiltshire and Hampstead, opened the eyes of Englishmen to the beauty of their countryside, rapidly being engulfed by Blake's 'Satanic Mills'. Even the French were astonished by the freshness of his vision, Delacroix himself repainting the background of his *Massacre at Chios* after seeing the Constables in the 1824 Salon.

His understanding of the structure of fields, woods and clouds, dovetails into the Lakeland poets' observation of nature. At his death, his friends, led by Beechey, presented *The Cornfield* to the National Gallery — an act of faith and courage at a time when Constable's true greatness was only just beginning to be realized. Reinagle's portrait was painted when the two young friends were spending the summer together in East Bergholt.

211 JAMES BARRY 1741-1806
Self-portrait, 1767

An *enfant terrible* of the late Georgians is here shown as a student in Rome, with two fellow artists in the background, Paine and Lefevre, and the *Torso Belvedere* faintly discernible behind. His fierce eye, gazing truculently at the spectator, forecasts a life of cantankerous quarrels ending with his expulsion from the Royal Academy. His obsession with the classics led him to vie with Benjamin West in the production of a *Death of Wolfe*, painted with figures in the nude. Apart from a series of paranoiac self-portraits, his most ambitious achievement was the decoration of the Great Room of the Society of Arts with *The Progress of Human Culture* (1777-83), characterized by ludicrous echoes of Michelangelo and Raphael.

Below

213 SAMUEL PALMER 1805-81
By George Richmond, 1829

A friend and fervent admirer of William Blake, Palmer's achievement was on a smaller scale. His best work, mainly romantic landscapes painted in tempera or water-colour, are associated with Shoreham, the little village in Kent where Palmer and his friends tried to capture the innocent life. *Hilly Scene with Church and Moon* (Tate Gallery), *The Magic Apple Tree* (Fitzwilliam Museum) and *Pastoral with Horse Chestnut* (Ashmolean Museum) belong to this period and are among his most exquisite works. Palmer's visionary appreciation of the English landscape became a formative influence in the art of Graham Sutherland.

212 WILLIAM BLAKE 1757-1827
By Thomas Phillips, 1807

Blake's genius as a mystic poet and author of *Songs of Innocence* and *Songs of Experience* overshadows his astonishing gifts as painter, engraver, illustrator and producer of illuminated books. From early childhood, when he saw angels in the sky, to his death singing with happiness, the pursuit of the visionary experience was his life's main theme. *Jerusalem* and *The Tiger*, two of the most familiar poems in the English language, can be read as the essence of this theme. Phillips is said to have caught the 'rapt poetic expression' on Blake's face by luring him to talk of his friendship with the Archangel Gabriel.

214 SIR MARC ISAMBARD BRUNEL 1769-1849
By Samuel Drummond, c.1835

One of the great figures in the history of civil engineering. He came of a family of Normandy farmers but took up his profession in America and Canada, where he practised as surveyor and architect and planned the defences of New York. In 1799 he came to England, married Sophia Kingdom, and devoted himself to inventing machinery, of which the most successful was a device for making ships' blocks, adopted eventually by the Royal Navy for Portsmouth Dockyard. However, his chief claim to fame was the design and construction of the Thames tunnel between Wapping and Rotherhithe. Disasters, floods, strikes and panic dogged the enterprise for nearly twenty years, but finally the tunnel was opened in 1843, though it cost Brunel two attacks of partial paralysis. The tunnel appears in the background of Drummond's portrait.

215 SIR RICHARD ARKWRIGHT 1732-92
By Joseph Wright of Derby, 1790

Arkwright came from a poor Lancashire family, but his inventive mind and his improvements in machinery for the manufacture of cotton led to his becoming High Sheriff of Derbyshire and one of the richest commoners in England. His application of water-power to spinning machinery still run by horse-power became one of the turning-points in the history of the factory system. The Gallery's portrait is a version of a whole-length still in the Arkwright family's possession, showing him sitting by a table on which is the spinning-jenny which revolutionized the cotton industry and indeed is a symbol of the whole Industrial Revolution.

216 JAMES WATT 1736-1819
By Carl von Breda, 1792

Watt began his working life as a scientific instrument maker for Glasgow University, where he observed the deficiencies of Newcomen's steam-engine and went on to patent his own steam-engine, in 1769, incorporating a special condenser and air-pump. The first practical cylindrical steam-engines were put on the market by Watt and his partner Matthew Boulton of Birmingham. The power thus generated replaced the old-fashioned horse- and water-driven machinery, almost immediately revolutionizing world industry and immortalizing Watt's name, inaccurately but effectively, as 'the inventor of the steam-engine'.

217 EDWARD JENNER 1749-1823
By James Northcote, 1803

Jenner is usually credited with the discovery of vaccination for smallpox, though in fact the principle had long been known in Turkey; indeed Lady Mary Wortley Montagu had had her own son inoculated there in 1717, and tried hard to introduce it to England on her return. Jenner observed the relationship between cowpox and smallpox among the dairymaids of his native Gloucestershire, experimented copiously and successfully with cowpox lymph and published his conclusions in 1798. The value of his work was recognized immediately, especially abroad, and by 1853 vaccination had become compulsory in England, and the dreaded smallpox reduced from a plague to occasional outbreaks.

218 WILLIAM WILBERFORCE 1759-1833
By Sir Thomas Lawrence, 1828

Wilberforce became MP for Hull in 1780,
devoting himself to social reform, especially in
criminal law. His interest in slavery abolition was
fired by James Ramsay, Thomas Clarkson and a
group of Quakers. Wilberforce himself took up
the cause in Parliament, ably assisted by his
friend Pitt, though fear of Jacobinism and the
bogy of the French Revolution led to several
defeats. Even the king was opposed to the
movement. Finally the Bill abolishing the British
slave-trade was passed in 1807, almost entirely
due to Wilberforce's convictions coupled with his
great charm and powers of persuasion.

219 ELIZABETH FRY (née GURNEY) 1780-1845
After Charles Robert Leslie

A member of a Norfolk Quaker family, she took
up the ministry after marriage and is said to have
melted the hardest of hearts with her preaching.
She became appalled at the condition of women
prisoners in Newgate, where overcrowding of
innocent and guilty alike was unbelievable. As a
visiting American minister said, 'the wretched
outcasts have been tamed and subdued by the
Christian eloquence of Mrs Fry', but it was her
introduction of a matron, proper supplies of
clothing and even a school that really helped. She
was also able to persuade the Government to
alleviate the hardships of prisoners enduring the
horrors of transportation.

Top row

220   Hannah More 1745-1833
By Augustin Edouart, 1827

Second row

221   Sir John Moore 1761-1809
By Sir Thomas Lawrence

**222   Robert Stewart, 2nd Marquess
of Londonderry (Lord Castlereagh)
1769-1822**
By Sir Thomas Lawrence

223   George Canning 1770-1827
By Sir Thomas Lawrence

Third row

224   George Romney 1734-1802
Self-portrait, 1782

**225   Sir Thomas Stamford Bingley
Raffles 1781-1826**
By George Francis Joseph, 1817

Fourth row

226   William Cobbett 1762-1835
By an unknown artist

227   Jane Austen 1775-1817
By Cassandra Austen (her sister),
c.1810

Fifth row

228   William Hazlitt 1778-1830
By William Bewick, 1822

229   John Clare 1793-1864
By William Hilton

230   Jeremy Bentham 1748-1832
By Henry William Pickersgill, 1829

Bottom row

231   Matthew Boulton 1728-1809
By an unknown artist

232   Sir Humphry Davy 1778-1829
By Thomas Phillips

THE VICTORIANS

The Victorian age was one of unprecedented change and progress. The technological revolution transformed Britain into a modern industrial nation, the workshop of the world and the centre of world trade, with a vast export market. With industrialization came the growth of large urban populations that radically altered the structure of British society. There were also appalling problems of poverty, disease and overcrowding. The extension of the suffrage meant the growth of popular democracy, and political parties were constantly reshaping to meet this new challenge. Scientific discoveries undermined traditional religious faith, and led to a crisis of doubt among the intelligentsia. The Victorians were inspired by the vision of progress in every sphere of life, the march of humanity towards higher goals, but became less certain of its achievement as the century progressed. Morality and high seriousness represent the temper of Victorian thought, leading sometimes to pomposity and hypocrisy, but endowing the great figures of the age with a heroic stature. A new mood of humanity and compassion paved the way to a genuine social consciousness and a desire to alleviate suffering.

Abroad, British naval supremacy remained unchallenged, and the Empire expanded, providing new markets for British goods and new sources of wealth. Numerous colonies were acquired through conquest, exploration and infiltration, requiring a professionally trained civil service to administer them, and British troops to protect their frontiers. The only serious threat to the peace of the Empire came with the Indian mutiny in 1857. Distrust of Russian ambitions in the East was a contributory factor to the outbreak of the Crimean War in 1854, the only major European conflict in which Britain became involved. In the last quarter of the nineteenth century the focus shifted to Africa, where Britain took over Egypt and the Sudan, acquired large tracts of territory further south, and came into conflict with the South African Boers.

Nearer at home the chief political challenges were posed by the issue of free trade versus protectionism, the intractable Irish problem, the rise of Chartism and trade unionism, and the increasing interference of the state in industrial, educational, health and social matters.

In the field of the arts there were many outstanding achievements. The novel, in the hands of Dickens, Thackeray, George Eliot and the Brontës, reached a high pinnacle of excellence. Tennyson, Browning and Matthew Arnold were all poets of the first rank. And at a lower level, popular literature reached out to a mass audience, in countless books, magazines and papers, which flourished as never before. The standard of Victorian painting is not always high, but there is an undeniable vitality to it, and a sense of excitement in the discovery of new subject-matter and styles. The cult of hero-worship and the intense interest in history and biography finds expression in countless portraits of famous figures. The advent of photography adds a new dimension to portraiture. The number and variety of surviving images enables the Victorians to be studied in much greater detail than the personalities of earlier periods.

233   QUEEN VICTORIA 1819-1901. Reigned 1837-1901
By Sir George Hayter, replica of his portrait of 1838

The young Victoria came to the throne on a wave of popular feeling. Her reign was the longest in British history, and so closely did she become identified with the attitudes and aspirations of her people that she gave her name to the period. This state portrait by her favourite court artist shows her in coronation robes, in a sumptuous setting, gazing idealistically upwards. The queen described a small version of the portrait as 'excessively like and beautifully painted'.

234 WILLIAM LAMB, 2nd VISCOUNT MELBOURNE 1779-1848
By John Partridge, 1844

Good-looking, talented, worldly and somewhat indolent by nature, Melbourne belonged to the group of influential Whig leaders. He was married to the beautiful and capricious Lady Caroline Lamb, who had a notorious affair with Byron. Melbourne became an MP in 1806, played a prominent part in the events leading to the passage of the Great Reform Bill, and succeeded Earl Grey as Prime Minister in 1834. He became an intimate friend and the guide and mentor of the young Queen Victoria. This close relationship ended with the queen's marriage, and Melbourne's resignation as Prime Minister in 1841. Partridge's portrait of the ageing statesman, dressed in a luxurious fur coat and seated in a study, is remarkably warm and sympathetic.

235 SIR ROBERT PEEL 1788-1850
By John Linnell, 1844

Peel was the leader of the Tory Party in succession to the Duke of Wellington. A man of commanding intelligence and integrity, he was the ablest statesman of his age. He was chief secretary for Ireland from 1812 to 1818, opposed Catholic emancipation, and established a police force, popularly called 'peelers'. He was later Home Secretary and the leader of the Tories in the House of Commons, and Prime Minister in 1841 and again from 1841 to 1846. Peel split his party by espousing the cause of free trade, because he believed that it was right for the country, thereby alienating the landowning class. This small cabinet picture by Linnell, better known as a landscapist, is full of vitality and character. Peel leans forward in his chair, a document in his hand, as if about to rise to his feet to speak. The setting emphasizes his role as a statesman and man of business.

236 QUEEN VICTORIA PRESENTING A BIBLE
By T. Jones Barker, c.1860

Queen Victoria is shown in the audience chamber at Windsor Castle,
presenting a Bible to a native prince. Neither the prince nor the
specific incident has yet been identified, but from his costume he is
probably of African origin. Beside the queen is her husband, Prince
Albert, and on the other side are Lord Palmerston and Lord John
Russell. The picture offers a fascinating commentary on imperialist
attitudes. The queen receives homage from her subject races, and in
return confers the benefits of religion and civilization.

237 QUEEN VICTORIA 1819-1901. Reigned 1837-1901
By Aaron Penley, c.1840

This charming water-colour was painted in the year of the queen's
marriage, and shows her beside a bust of her husband, Prince Albert.
Her marriage to her cousin, son of the Duke of Saxe-Coburg-Gotha,
aroused hostility, but Albert's devotion to duty, public-spiritedness,
and interest in art and technology marked him as an outstanding
public figure. The Great Exhibition of 1851 was largely his brainchild.
He and Victoria were a devoted couple, and admirable parents with a
large family. Albert's early death in 1861 was a shattering blow from
which Victoria only slowly recovered.

239 CHARLES DICKENS 1812-70
By Daniel Maclise, 1830

A portrait of the young Dickens, commissioned for the engraved frontispiece of *Nicholas Nickleby*. Since *Pickwick Papers*, Dickens's success had been phenomenal. This portrait by his close friend, the Irish artist Maclise, is certainly idealized, showing the novelist looking up at the light for inspiration; but it also captures his magnetism, dandyism and sheer animal energy.

238 THE BRONTË SISTERS
By Patrick Branwell Brontë, c.1834

This is one of the most famous pictures in the Gallery, although it is of little artistic merit. Apart from a drawing of Charlotte and a fragment from another group of Emily, it is the only surviving representation of the three famous sisters, who were among the greatest novelists of the age. Anne (1820-49) is shown on the left, Emily (1818-48) in the centre and Charlotte (1816-55) on the right. Below the pillar the painted-out figure of Branwell can just be made out. The portrait conveys something of the intense and haunting atmosphere of Haworth Parsonage. It was seen by Charlotte's biographer, Mrs Gaskell, who commented on the cropped hair of the girls, and their 'sad dreamy-looking eyes'. The portrait was found folded up on top of a wardrobe after the death of Charlotte's husband. Its survival seems to have been a matter of chance.

240 JENNY LIND 1820-87
By Edward Magnus, replica of his portrait of 1846

Jenny Lind, the 'Swedish nightingale', was one of the most popular and beloved singers of her time. Beautiful and intelligent, she conveyed through her voice — a brilliant soprano — the charm of her personality. This portrait was painted the year before her sensational London debut.

241 ROBERT BROWNING 1812-89
By Michele Gordigiani, 1858

Browning was one of the greatest and most original poets of the Victorian period, pre-eminent for his intellectuality, and for his use of psychological monologues. He had caused a considerable stir by eloping with Elizabeth Barrett in 1846, and they had lived an idyllically happy existence in Florence since then. This portrait and the companion one of Elizabeth (see below) were painted by a local Florentine artist. W.M. Rossetti described the portrait of Robert in an article of 1890: 'The spacious unwrinkled forehead, in which thought seems to have accumulated and condensed; the watchful eyes, slightly over-drooped by their lids; the half-smiling, half-pondering mouth, — Browning's face was, indeed, seldom without a certain lambency, as of pleasant and kindly thought, which would easily lapse into a smile'.

242 ELIZABETH BARRETT BROWNING 1806-61
By Michele Gordigiani, 1858

This is a pair to the portrait of Robert Browning reproduced above. Elizabeth was for many years more highly considered as a writer than her husband; her love lyrics were especially popular. Their marriage was intensely happy, and her early death from tuberculosis dealt Browning a devastating blow. This portrait by Gordigiani conveys Elizabeth's physical frailty and her soulful and romantic looks.

243 THOMAS BABINGTON, LORD MACAULAY
1800-59
By Edward Matthew Ward, 1853

Macaulay was one of the intellectual giants of the early
Victorian period. His famous *History of England*, on
which he laboured from 1839, became a classic in his
lifetime. He was also a prolific essayist and a popular
poet. He led an active political career, becoming an MP
in 1830, serving on the supreme council of India,
1834-8, and as Secretary of War, 1839-41. The portrait
is a charming interior scene showing Macaulay in his
chambers at Albany surrounded by his familiar
possessions. He complained that the artist had poisoned
him with the smell of paint, and had made him look
'uglier than a daguerreotype'.

244 THOMAS CARLYLE 1795-1881
By Sir John Everett Millais, 1877

Carlyle was a formidable thinker and historian. In his
prolific writings he eulogized heroes and strong
governments like those of Cromwell and Frederick the
Great. He mistrusted technological progress, and
analysed brilliantly the sufferings of the common
people. Popularly called the 'Sage of Chelsea', his
corrosive criticism and uncertain temper became
legendary. The portrait of him by Millais was
commissioned by the historian, J.A. Froude, who wrote
of the second sitting: '...under Millais' hand the old
Carlyle stood again upon the canvas as I had not seen
him for thirty years. The secret of the inner features
had been evidently caught'.

245   SIR EDWIN LANDSEER 1802-73
By John Ballantyne, c.1865

Landseer was one of the most popular painters of the Victorian period, famous for his imaginative pictures of dogs and stags, often imitating human emotions and actions. He was a favourite painter at court, and the countless thousands of engravings after his works ensured him a vast audience. He is shown in this picture in Baron Marochetti's studio, working on one of the lions which he modelled for the base of Nelson's column in Trafalgar Square. Landseer was furious with Ballantyne when this picture was exhibited in 1865 without his permission, since it revealed his designs for the lions before they had even been cast in bronze. Ballantyne was forced to withdraw the work from an exhibition of pictures by him of artists in their studios.

246   JOHN RUSKIN 1819-1900
By Hubert von Herkomer, 1879

Ruskin was the greatest English Victorian art critic. His voluminous writings profoundly influenced contemporary attitudes to art, architecture and aesthetics. Among his more important works are *Modern Painters* (1843-60), *Seven Lamps of Architecture* (1849) and *The Stones of Venice* (1851-3). In later life he turned to social and political problems, advocating socialistic reforms which alienated many of his earlier admirers. He was keenly interested in science, and was himself a talented water-colourist. Herkomer, an artist of German origin, described the sittings for this portrait at Ruskin's house in Denmark Hill: 'in the little garret bedroom which had formerly been his nursery ... whilst sitting he was theorising about the methods of painting'. Ruskin admired the portrait, saying it was the first 'that has ever given what good may be gleaned out of the clods of my face'.

247 CHARLES ROBERT DARWIN 1809-82
By the Hon John Collier, replica of his portrait of 1881

No scientist had a more revolutionary impact on Victorian attitudes than Darwin. His theory of evolution destroyed the old biblical myths about the creation of the world, and seemed to put man on the same footing as the apes. Darwin was accused of undermining traditional religious faith, and his ideas were fiercely attacked. Like other theories that radically alter man's view of the world, the theory of evolution appeared obvious once it had been discovered. But it needed a genius like Darwin to conceive and demonstrate it. The portrait here shows Darwin at the very end of his life, when he had become a venerable and bearded sage. Even so there remains more than a glimmer of the intellectual power and passion for truth that led him on his famous voyage in the *Beagle*.

248 THOMAS HENRY HUXLEY 1825-95
By the Hon John Collier, 1883

Huxley was one of the best-known and most influential scientists of his day. A firm supporter of Darwin's theory of evolution, he battled throughout his career against prejudice and obscurantism. His early publications on the relationship between man and other forms of life were widely read. He was often involved in controversy, for many of his ideas were in violent opposition to accepted religious teaching. Through his fearless championship of the spirit of free enquiry and his formidable analytical powers, he helped to educate public opinion to the momentous changes taking place in scientific thought. Huxley carried out important researches on fish, reptiles and birds, but he is best remembered as a scientific popularizer and spokesman. He was a prolific writer and lecturer, took an active interest in the Royal School of Mines, sat on the first school board for London, and served on numerous royal commissions. This sensitive portrait by his son-in-law shows him skull in hand, elbow resting on weighty tomes, as if in the act of delivering a lecture.

249 ALFRED, LORD TENNYSON 1809-92
By George Frederic Watts, c.1863-4

This is a memorable portrait of perhaps the greatest English poet of the age. The lyricism and psychological intensity of Tennyson's early work were later modified into a more public poetry. In his various portraits of the poet Watts sought to embody 'the shape and colour of a mind and life', and nowhere more prophetically than in this picture. The head has the mysterious and brooding presence of an icon, while the bay leaves behind are symbolic of the poet's vocation.

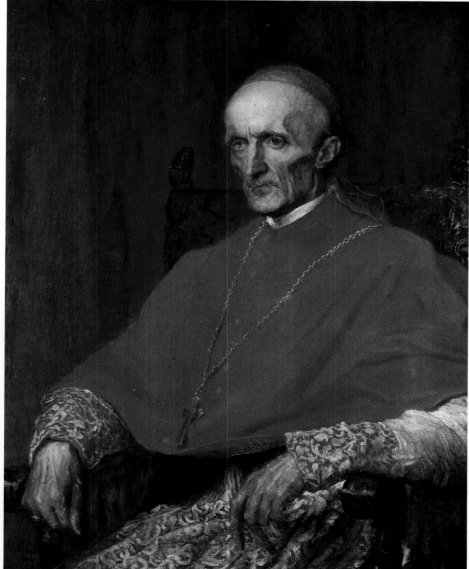

250 CARDINAL HENRY MANNING 1808-92
By George Frederic Watts, 1884

Manning was Archbishop of Westminster and leader of the Roman Catholic Church in England. He is shown here in one of Watts's most impressive portraits, deriving from a Renaissance formula for the portraits of popes. Manning was originally an Anglican archdeacon, but he was converted to Roman Catholicism during the heady days of the Oxford Movement. He was an ecclesiastical statesman of outstanding ability and a brilliant preacher. Because of his inspiring influence and subtlety of mind he was much feared and disliked in the Anglican Church, By temperament he was ascetic and austere, qualities on which Watts seizes with powerful effect. The bony face has a gaunt, skull-like appearance. The colour scheme of reds intensifies the sense of mortality. The spirit alone remains unconquered.

251 WILLIAM MORRIS 1834-96
By George Frederic Watts, 1870

Artist and designer, poet and socialist, founder of the famous firm of Morris & Co and of the Kelmscott Press, there seems no end to Morris's interests and enthusiasms. Appalled by the standard of contemporary craftsmanship and design, he founded his own firm for the production of highly original and hand-produced furniture, wallpapers, fabrics, stained glass and other decorative items. He had a revolutionary impact on Victorian taste and design. He was also an outstanding poet, delighting in the sagas and stories of the classical period and the middle ages. His imagery is powerful and his use of language blunt and condensed. Later in life Morris became obsessed by the underlying evils of contemporary society, and espoused his own form of idealistic socialism.

252   FLORENCE NIGHTINGALE (1820-1910) at Scutari
By Jerry Barrett, c.1856

Few people came out of the Crimean War with credit,
but Florence Nightingale's campaign on behalf of the sick
and wounded was one of the great achievements. The
British Army had gone to war with Russia in the Crimea
in 1854 poorly equipped. Disease and cold quickly
wrought havoc, and the hospitals became hopelessly
overcrowded and insanitary. With a party of nurses, and
in the teeth of official opposition, Florence Nightingale
went out to remedy this situation, establishing herself at
Scutari, one of the British bases. Her work in the
hospitals there totally transformed them, and laid the
foundations of the modern nursing system. The picture
by Barrett is a sketch for a large work showing her
greeting the sick and wounded at the gates of Scutari.

253   SIR RICHARD BURTON 1821-90
By Frederic, Lord Leighton, c.1872-5

Burton was a famous explorer, author, and translator,
whose exploits in Africa and the Middle East earned him
a legendary reputation. The portrait of him by Leighton,
a friend and admirer, conveys a strong sense of Burton's
intense and demonic personality. The scar on the left
cheek and the short cropped hair accentuate the effect of
the dominant, arching eyebrows, and the threatening,
fiery eyes. The portrait was begun shortly after Burton
had been sacked as British consul in Damascus. 'Don't
make me ugly, there's a good fellow', he told the artist.
The picture was exhibited at the Academy in 1875, but
Burton never acquired it, so perhaps he did not approve
of the likeness.

254 HORATIO, 1st EARL KITCHENER OF KHARTOUM 1850-1916
By Hubert von Herkomer, 1890

Kitchener was the epitome of the successful imperialist general. He served under Wolseley in the relief expedition to Gordon in Khartoum, and subsequently commanded armies in Egypt and the Sudan. Kitchener's reputation for invincibility was enhanced later by his victories during the Boer War. He made the transition from active command in the field to military administration with great aplomb. It was he who was chiefly responsible for converting the small British Army into a military machine of three million men during the early years of the First World War. The portrait by Herkomer was painted soon after a successful campaign against the Dervishes, and stresses Kitchener's stern and commanding qualities as a leader.

255 CAPTAIN FREDERICK BURNABY 1842-85
By James Tissot, 1870

Burnaby's exploits as a cavalry officer and explorer captured every schoolboy's imagination. Over six feet four inches tall, he was reputed to be the strongest man in the British Army. His books about his adventures, including *A Ride to Khiva* (1876) and *On Horseback through Asia Minor* (1877), were best-sellers. In 1885 he took part in the relief expedition to Khartoum in the Sudan, and died from a spear wound. Tissot was a French artist who became famous for his scenes of fashionable life. This portrait admirably conveys the character of the nonchalant, impeccably-dressed Burnaby, smoking a cigarette, in a most attractive, aesthetic interior.

256 HENRY TEMPLE, 3rd VISCOUNT PALMERSTON 1784-1865
By Frederick Cruikshank, c.1855

Palmerston was a dominating figure in British politics for over fifty years. He was a supporter and friend of Canning, but later joined the Whigs. As Foreign Secretary, 1831-41 and again 1846-51, he raised British prestige to unparalleled heights by a mixture of craft, bluster and force. He was largely responsible for establishing the new state of Belgium, rescued Turkey from Russian designs, interfered in Spain on behalf of Queen Isabella, went to war with China, stamped on the slave trade, and compelled Greece to come to terms in the Don Pacifico affair. He became Prime Minister in 1855, brought the Crimean War to a successful conclusion, and signed an advantageous peace. His political position thereafter was virtually unassailable. This portrait, painted at the zenith of his power and influence, relates to a full-length work showing him in the House of Lords.

257 DINNER AT HADDO HOUSE, SEPTEMBER 1884
By Alfred Edward Emslie

This picture shows a scene in the dining-room of the Scottish home of the Earl and Countess of Aberdeen. Prominent among the guests at the end of the table, to the right of Lady Aberdeen, is the veteran statesman and then Prime Minister, William Ewart Gladstone (1809-98), who was on a tour of Scotland. To the left of Lady Aberdeen is Lord Rosebery, who succeeded Gladstone as Prime Minister. Other guests include Mrs Gladstone and Lady Rosebery, Professor Henry Drummond, the Earl and Countess of Elgin, Robert Farquharson, MP, and G.W. Smalley. It was a custom at Haddo for guests to be regaled with bagpipe music, the piper shown here being Andrew Cant. The picture not only records an important occasion, but is a charming view of social life in the mid-1880s.

258   JOSEPH CHAMBERLAIN (1836-1914) AND ARTHUR JAMES BALFOUR, 1st EARL OF BALFOUR (1848-1930)
By Sydney Prior Hall, c.1895

This is a rare and informal view of two great statesmen, lounging back on one of the green front benches in the House of Commons, evidently taking part in a debate. S.P. Hall, special artist on the *Graphic* for over thirty years, was adept at recording events and personalities instantaneously. A huge collection of his drawings belongs to the Gallery. Though undated, this picture was probably painted in the mid-1890s, from sketches made on the spot. Chamberlain, formidable political boss of Birmingham, had deserted the Liberal Party over the issue of Irish home rule. He joined Lord Salisbury's third administration in 1895 as Secretary of State for the Colonies. The intellectual Balfour, Salisbury's nephew, and leader of the Tories in the House of Commons, succeeded his uncle as Prime Minister in 1902.

259   BENJAMIN DISRAELI, EARL OF BEACONSFIELD 1804-81
By Sir John Everett Millais, 1881

Few who knew the young Disraeli, with his restless and romantic character, could have predicted his transformation into a great statesman. His Jewish background and insatiable ambition alienated many, but he gradually asserted his influence on the Tory Party through his outstanding abilities as a politician and orator, becoming Prime Minister in 1868. He guided the passage of the second Reform Bill, and his diplomatic triumphs included the purchase of the Suez Canal and the Congress of Berlin. He wrote several brilliant political novels, including *Coningsby* (1844) and *Lothair* (1870). This portrait was painted in the last months of his life, when he was already frail. Disraeli himself commented: 'I suppose it is vanity, which seems absurd at my time of life with my broken appearance, but it must be pardonable to wish to be painted by the greatest portrait painter in England...'.

260 ELLEN TERRY (1847-1928) as Lady Macbeth
By John Singer Sargent, 1889
(On loan from the Tate Gallery)

Born into a theatrical family, Ellen Terry first went on stage at the age of nine. In 1864, at the age of sixteen, she married G.F. Watts, an artist thirty years her senior, who immortalized her in a series of lyrical pictures, including *Choosing* (front cover). They separated within a year, and, after living for a time with the architect E.W. Godwin, Ellen Terry returned to the stage. In 1867 she began her remarkable partnership with Henry Irving at the Lyceum, playing with him in a wide range of Shakespearian and other classic plays. Her beauty and vitality as much as her acting ability made her the leading actress of the period. Sargent's picture records one of her celebrated roles, as Lady Macbeth. The artist attended the opening performance on 29 December 1888, and was bowled over both by the actress and her stunning butterfly dress. 'Miss Terry has just come out in Lady Macbeth and looks magnificent in it', he wrote, 'but she has not yet made up her mind to let me paint her in one of the dresses until she is quite convinced that she is a success. From a pictorial point of view there can be no doubt about it — magenta hair!'

Above left
261 AUBREY BEARDSLEY 1872-98
By Jacques-Emile Blanche, 1895

In a short life of intense and fevered activity, and despite — or perhaps because of — the ill health which dogged him from childhood, Beardsley produced an enormous quantity of brilliant, original and highly-finished black-and-white drawings. His illustrations for the *Yellow Book* and the *Savoy* attracted attention and aroused furious controversy. The drawings were strange — often morbid or erotic. His work included designs for *The Rape of the Lock*, for Oscar Wilde's *Salome* and for Ernest Dowson's *Pierrot of the Minute*. As well as a brilliantly accomplished artist and draughtsman, Beardsley was immensely erudite, musically gifted and a conversationalist of mannered elegance and charm. He was received into the Roman Catholic Church shortly before his death, from consumption, at Mentone.

Above
262 SIR HENRY IRVING 1838-1905
By Jules Bastien-Lepage, 1880

Irving dominated the London stage for the last thirty years of Victoria's reign. Born John Henry Brodribb, he worked as a clerk in London, and studied elocution to overcome a stutter. During the 1860s he achieved success on the London stage, and in 1867 played for the first time with Ellen Terry, the start of a long and memorable partnership. Irving established his reputation as a tragedian with his *Hamlet* at the Lyceum in 1874. His style was individual and controversial, but its power and intensity kept audiences spellbound. A great manager as well as actor, Irving made several American and Canadian tours, received many honours, and was the first actor to be knighted (1895). This portrait was given to the Gallery by Ellen Terry in 1910.

263 OSCAR WILDE 1856-1900
By Carlo Pellegrini ('Ape'), 1884

Wilde was a brilliant dramatist, a poet, and a cult figure in the aesthetic movement. His unconventional behaviour, witty and paradoxical remarks, and dandified pose as a devotee of art and beauty, earned him notoriety. His first volume of poems was published in 1881, and in 1884 he made a sensational tour of the United States, complete with aesthetic rig. In the 1890s he wrote a series of scintillating comedies, including *The Importance of Being Earnest*. His conviction for homosexual offences and subsequent imprisonment marked the tragic and pathetic end to one of the great literary talents of the late nineteenth century. This caricature by the Italian artist Pellegrini was published in the society magazine *Vanity Fair*.

264   SIR WILLIAM SCHWENK GILBERT 1836-1911
By Frank Holl, 1886

Gilbert wrote numerous plays, sketches and stories, but his name is irrevocably linked with that of Sir Arthur Sullivan, for whose music he wrote the libretti of the 'Savoy' comic operas. His wit, skilled precision as satirist and versifier and the deft marriage of his words with Sullivan's music combined to produce such popular and apparently timeless successes as *HMS Pinafore* (1878), *Iolanthe* (1882), *The Mikado* (1885) and *The Yeomen of the Guard* (1888). Though the partnership lasted over twenty years, it was never an easy or a very happy one. Gilbert was irascible, quarrels became increasingly frequent, and after *The Gondoliers* (1889) he and Sullivan parted. They occasionally collaborated later, but never approached the popularity of their earlier operas. Gilbert built the Garrick Theatre with the profits from his plays, and was knighted in 1907.

265   SIR ARTHUR SULLIVAN 1842-1900
By Sir John Everett Millais, 1888

Sullivan achieved early success as a composer of serious music, but in 1866 he wrote *Cox and Box*, a comic operetta, and in 1871 he collaborated for the first time with W.S. Gilbert, on *Thespis*. This marked the start of a long, stormy and prolific partnership. With Gilbert as librettist, Sullivan composed a series of triumphantly successful comic operas, which were performed, after 1881, in the Savoy Theatre, built specially for them by Richard d'Oyly Carte. The huge success of the 'Savoy' operas continually frustrated Sullivan's longing to devote more time to serious music. He composed numerous songs, orchestral and sacred pieces and one grand opera, *Ivanhoe* (1891), but with the exception of his setting of *The Lost Chord*, these are seldom heard now. This portrait and that of Gilbert (above) were bequeathed to the Gallery by the respective sitters.

THE TWENTIETH CENTURY

The history of the first half of the twentieth century is one of rapid advances in science and technology, two shattering world wars, and economic and social revolution. In Britain, from the long-drawn-out summer of Queen Victoria's reign, the Empire was ushered into its final years under Edward VII and the country enjoyed the brief period of gaiety and elegance which still bears his name. Already, however, there were strong forces at work beneath the apparently assured and prosperous surface. Pressure for home rule in Ireland, a difficult political and economic situation at home and ominous tremors from Europe were key factors during the early years of George V's reign. All these problems were engulfed in the holocaust of the First World War, but re-emerged before the last treaty had been signed.

The revolutionary movements in the arts which had spread from Paris and elsewhere found eager adherents in a younger generation of artists, musicians and writers. Vorticism was perhaps the first genuine effort by a group of British artists to associate themselves independently with an international movement. The First World War left a generation disillusioned by the wholesale slaughter of relatives, friends and heroes, and the mood of the country often degenerated into frivolity in the period aptly known as the 'Roaring Twenties'. Intellectual and artistic life in Britain was dominated for the first twenty-five years by that close-knit group of kindred souls (and relatives), the Bloomsbury group. Although associates of the group produced a number of interesting painters and writers, certain figures like Maynard Keynes, Virginia Woolf and Bertrand Russell tower above their fellows. Keynes it was who helped to formulate the economic thinking which was slowly to drag the country out of the bleak years of depression, although even this process was halted by the outbreak of hostilities in 1939. The Second World War seems to have brought out the best in people, and certainly the country had not for a long time been as united as it was under politicians of the calibre of Churchill and military leaders such as Montgomery.

Post-war life has seen a slow but sure recovery, with economic and consequent social changes which would have seemed impossible at the beginning of the century. Scientific developments in communications, transport and industry which were the wonders of the pre-war world are now everyday commonplaces. Even in the visual arts and music, where Britain had for so long lagged behind the rest of Europe, there has been a revival of exceptional vigour which has raised London to a major cultural centre for the world.

As regards portraiture, the camera has entirely relieved the artist of his function as simple recorder of appearances. From this point of view, the field has become wide open, and the National Portrait Gallery can collect archival material on an unprecedented scale for the enlightenment of future generations. Portraits, however, continue to be painted and sculpted, often with a new artistic freedom which provides a unique chronicle of the creative relationship between sitter and artist.

281   THE ROYAL FAMILY AT BUCKINGHAM PALACE, 1913
By Sir John Lavery
(By courtesy of H.I. Spottiswoode)

This imposing group shows George V (1865-1936; reigned 1910-36) and Queen Mary (1867-1953) with their eldest children, the Prince of Wales (the future Duke of Windsor; 1894-1972) and Princess Mary (1897-1965). It was commissioned by the printer, W.H. Spottiswoode, for presentation to the nation, and shows the family somewhat dwarfed by the splendours of the White Drawing Room at Buckingham Palace. Perhaps the last successful grand state image of the British monarchy, it is, despite its intentional reference to Velazquez, comparatively modern in feeling.

282 THE THREE DAUGHTERS OF EDWARD VII
By Sydney Prior Hall, 1883

Among what one art historian has described as the 'series of nonentities' employed by Queen Victoria in her search for portrait painters who offered the best value for money, Sydney Prior Hall is often noteworthy for the genuine charm he brings to his subjects. This portrait of her three daughters, commissioned by Queen Alexandra, is no exception. From left to right, the princesses are: Victoria (1868-1935); Maud (1869-1938), who later became Queen of Norway; and Louise (1867-1931), Princess Royal and later Duchess of Fife. Painted in the same year as Seurat's *Une Baignade à Asnières*, the picture is a relic of an earlier era, as indeed were its subjects, who lived almost until the Second World War.

283 EDWARD VII 1841-1910. Reigned 1901-10
By Sir Luke Fildes, 1912, replica of his portrait of 1902

Fildes's imperial image was the first state portrait to be exhibited at the Royal Academy after the dearth of portraits during Queen Victoria's widowhood. As such it aroused a lot of popular interest at the time, although today it appears rather dull as a painting, and, as an image, slightly ridiculous in its pomposity. A long-serving Prince of Wales, Edward VII was supremely conscious of his position and responsibilities as king and emperor. The portrait, based on a long tradition of regal images from Henry VIII to Napoleon, reflects his new role. This copy was presented to the Gallery by his son, George V.

284   DAVID LLOYD GEORGE, 1st EARL LLOYD-GEORGE 1863-1945
By Sir William Orpen, 1927

This portrait of the famous Liberal statesman was originally a private commission, but it was refused on completion and remained in Orpen's possession until his death. Although it now seems a fairly conventional likeness, it was at the time an informal type of pose for a portrait of a leading politician. The scattered papers on the table and the sitter's expression of inspiration suggest rather an absent-minded philosopher. In fact Orpen is successful in catching the blend of idealism and sound common sense which characterized Lloyd George's distinguished career, and it was apparently a pose he habitually assumed when working.

285   ARTHUR NEVILLE CHAMBERLAIN 1869-1940
By Henry Lamb, 1939

Lamb's portrait of Chamberlain was the result of a commission from a group of supporters in his constituency in Birmingham. Ironically enough it was not begun until early in 1939, after Chamberlain's agreement with Hitler at Munich which has done so much to damage his subsequent reputation. The portrait reflects a measure of the anxiety of the days leading up to the declaration of war. The artist remembered that during a sitting on the day following the occupation of Poland, in response to his remark that there was not much to enjoy in the picture yet, Chamberlain replied in a 'voice of ashes': 'The time for enjoyment has gone by'.

Below

286 AUGUSTUS JOHN 1878-1961
Self-portrait, c.1900

This forceful self-portrait is a typically brilliant drawing by perhaps the best-known British artist of the first half of the century. John's picturesque Bohemianism and dazzling portraits of the social world ensured that he was seldom out of the public eye. This is one of his most lively and arrogant statements about himself.

287 DAVID HERBERT LAWRENCE 1885-1930
By Jan Juta, 1920

This icon-like image of the famous novelist was painted by the South African-born artist Jan Juta while he was in Sardinia, working with Lawrence on the illustrations for the first edition of *Sea and Sardinia*. Lawrence's enigmatic personality and mystical outlook seem to have provoked rather eccentric portraits, none of them of great distinction. Juta sees him as a Rasputin-like prophet gazing appropriately into the future. Lawrence's novels were indeed prophetic and provoked considerable hostility at the time.

288 GWEN JOHN 1876-1939
Self-portrait, c.1900

Painted about the same time as Augustus John's self-portrait drawing (plate 286), this portrait shows that Gwen shared not only physical traits with her brother, but a good deal of his pride and defiant independence as well. After studying at the Slade School with Augustus under Henry Tonks, she spent most of her life in Paris, living in great poverty. Although she led a recluse-like existence she numbered the sculptor Rodin and the great German poet Rilke among her friends and admirers. Virtually unknown in her lifetime, the subtle technique and colouring and quiet atmosphere of her small paintings and drawings have subsequently won her higher critical approval than her brother.

289   RUPERT BROOKE 1887-1915
By Clara Ewald, 1911

This unfamiliar image of the popular poet who met a tragic death in the First World War was only rediscovered in 1972, when the artist's son presented it to the Gallery. It was painted early in 1911 in Munich, where Brooke was staying after taking his BA at Cambridge. Frau Ewald kept more or less open house for Cambridge students and decided to paint him, 'partly, perhaps to cheer him up'. The hat was not typical and belonged to the artist's son. Although Brooke's Cambridge contemporaries were divided in their opinions of the portrait they agreed that it gave a good idea of his fresh and vivid colour which no photograph could convey.

290   JAMES JOYCE 1862-1941
By Jacques-Emile Blanche, 1935

It is always a surprise to find the author of the revolutionary novel, *Ulysses*, looking here rather more like the head of a successful family business. Blanche's urbane image, however, is slightly misleading, for he himself is full of amusing anecdotes concerning the Irish novelist's eccentricities, in his reminiscences, *More Portraits of a Lifetime*. Blanche met Joyce through 'les Amis de 1914', an arts society in Paris where both were living at the time. Joyce expressed a desire to sit to Blanche but was particular that he should not be painted full-face, as he was self-conscious about the very heavy lenses of his spectacles.

291 JOHN MAYNARD KEYNES, BARON KEYNES 1883-1943
By Gwen Raverat, c.1908

After his distinguished undergraduate career at Cambridge, Keynes worked for a time in the India Office, and through his friendships with Duncan Grant and Lytton Strachey became a leading member of the Bloomsbury group. This fresh and lively portrait of the young economist was drawn during this period by one of Vanessa Bell's painter friends, Gwen Darwin, who was later to become Keynes's sister-in-law and to marry the artist Jacques Raverat. Keynes himself went on to become the greatest economist of the century. His theories had a profound effect on economic thought and the control of unemployment throughout the non-communist world.

292 LYTTON STRACHEY 1880-1932
By Simon Bussy, 1904

The publication of *Eminent Victorians* in 1918 marked the arrival of a bright new talent on the literary scene and inaugurated a new type of biography. Lytton Strachey's name has since become synonymous with the Bloomsbury group, although this portrait is the work of an artist who was not strictly a member. Simon Bussy was a French post-impressionist, who wooed and married Strachey's sister Dorothy, rather to the family's alarm, in 1903. This masterly study of the young writer at work was probably drawn while Strachey was visiting the Bussys at their villa in the South of France in April 1904.

293 BERTRAND RUSSELL, LORD RUSSELL 1872-1970
By Roger Fry, c.1923

Bertrand Russell's reputation as one of the leading minds of the century was secured with the publication of *Principia Mathematica* (with A.N. Whitehead) in 1910. A Fellow of Trinity College, Cambridge, and an associate of the Bloomsbury group, his first published work had appeared in 1896. Roger Fry considered him 'one of the men of genius of our time' and has clearly tried to capture a feeling of his great intellect.

Above
294 EDWARD MORGAN FORSTER 1879-1970
By Dora Carrington, after 1924

Although E.M. Forster was not yet fifty when this portrait was painted, it was after the publication of his last novel, *A Passage to India*. His reputation has continued to rest on this and on *Howard's End*, and he remains one of the most widely read and influential of modern novelists. The portrait seems to have been produced secretly during Forster's weekend visits to Carrington's home, Ham Spray House, before she tragically committed suicide in 1932. Forster was apparently unaware that it was being painted and suspected it must have taken a long time.

295 ROGER ELIOT FRY 1866-1934
Self-portrait, c.1930-4

Fry the artist is not perhaps as well known as Fry the critic and art historian. His writings, especially *Vision and Design* (1920) and *Transformations* (1926), exercised the greatest influence on public taste since Ruskin, and he was certainly responsible for the general distaste for Victorian art and architecture until the 1950s.

296   HUGH GAITSKELL 1906-63
By Judy Cassab, 1957

By the time Hugh Gaitskell sat for this striking portrait, he had already
been leader of the Labour Party for two years, the youngest ever leader of
a political party, at forty-nine. Earlier, he had also set a record as youngest
chancellor of the exchequer, in Attlee's Government in 1950. His rivalry
with Nye Bevan, both over Labour economic policy and for the leadership
of the party, was one of the great factors of political life in the 1950s.
During the controversy he raised over Clause 4 of the Labour Party
constitution about common ownership it seemed unlikely that his career
would survive. By the time of his premature death two years later, it was
generally agreed, however, that the country had lost its most promising
politician and future prime minister. The artist was born in Hungary and
has spent most of her life in Australia.

**297   WILLIAM MAXWELL AITKEN, LORD
BEAVERBROOK 1879-1964**
By Walter Richard Sickert, 1935

Sickert's habit of painting many of his later works from
press photographs and snapshots resulted not only in
some of the most original works of art produced in
Britain between the wars but also in a number of unlikely
but now much admired portraits. This monumental
image of the Canadian-born press baron and statesman
(it is nearly six feet high), was one of a series of portraits
of friends painted for Sir James Dunn. Like the Royal
Academy, that year, Sir James refused to accept it and it
was bought by Beaverbrook for the *Daily Express* offices.
It was worked up from a snapshot to which Sickert
added a background from St Peter's, Thanet, where he
lived but which Beaverbrook had never visited.

298 CLEMENTINE OGILVY, LADY SPENCER-CHURCHILL 1885-1977
By Sir John Lavery, c.1915

Following the disastrous Gallipoli landing, and his subsequent resignation from the Admiralty in 1915, Winston Churchill was 'forced to remain a spectator of tragedy' until he decided to rejoin the Army at the end of the year. During the six months he was out of effective office, he was persuaded by his wife and the fashionable portrait painter, John Lavery, to take up painting. This elegant little sketch of Mrs Churchill and her year-old daughter Sarah is thought to have been painted while Lavery was holidaying with the Churchills at Hoe Farm, Godalming. During this time, Lavery and Churchill both painted portraits of each other at the easel.

299 SIR WINSTON CHURCHILL 1874-1965
By Walter Richard Sickert, 1927

This informal and relatively youthful image of the great statesman was painted in Sickert's studio at 27 Highbury Place in 1927. It was the year following the General Strike, during which Churchill's role as Chancellor of the Exchequer had not been an entirely happy one. Despite its relaxed air, there is a profound feeling of thoughtfulness behind Churchill's expression, a factor which may have contributed to its not finding favour with the family. Later events were to show again that Churchill preferred a more heroic and commanding view of himself. Unlike Sickert's later portraits, the Churchill is based on a drawing from life. It provides a revealing glimpse at an early stage in his career of the man who almost single-handed was to lead a nation to victory.

300 CONVERSATION PIECE AT ROYAL LODGE, WINDSOR
By Sir James Gunn, 1950

Commissioned by the Trustees of the National Portrait Gallery, this charming group shows George VI (1895-1952; reigned 1936-52), Queen Elizabeth (the Queen Mother), and the then Princess Elizabeth at tea in the Royal Lodge with Princess Margaret about to take her seat. While almost self-consciously emulating the eighteenth-century conversation piece of Zoffany and Arthur Devis, it is nevertheless an accurate and valuable record of the much-loved family it portrays and of its period. Both the king's cigarette and the royal corgi are details which have already passed into history.

301 QUEEN ELIZABETH THE QUEEN MOTHER born 1900
By Sir Gerald Kelly, c.1938

The commission for state portraits of George VI and Queen Elizabeth after the coronation fell in 1938 to Sir Gerald Kelly, an artist renowned for his painstaking industry and integrity. This gracious image of one of the best-loved members of the royal family was a study produced in connection with the full-length state portrait, now at Windsor. It cleverly combines a sense of familiarity with a distinctly regal air by showing Queen Elizabeth in a familiar pose, half smiling, and at the same time adopting a very low viewpoint.

302 EDWARD, DUKE OF WINDSOR (Edward VIII) 1894-1972
By Sir James Gunn, 1954

From being a highly popular Prince of Wales, noted both for his informality and for his concern with social problems, the Duke of Windsor rapidly dropped out of the public eye after his abdication and marriage. James Gunn's sketch catches something of the sadness of the duke's years in exile, in an expression of wistfulness which is totally free of any undertone of bitterness. It was painted at the Windsors' home in Paris, in connection with a double portrait.

303   HER MAJESTY QUEEN ELIZABETH II born 1926
By Pietro Annigoni, 1970

It is generally agreed that Annigoni's first portrait of the Queen,
commissioned by the Fishmongers' Company in 1954, is the best yet to
have been painted of her. Aloof and slightly disdainful in a Ruritanian
landscape, it is a romantic image of genuine charm. His second portrait,
commissioned for the National Portrait Gallery by Mr Hugh Leggatt in
1970, is far more serious in tone — reflecting perhaps something of the
cares and responsibilities of the monarchy. It offers an alternative
solution to the problems of creating a royal portrait in the twentieth
century.

304 BENJAMIN BRITTEN, LORD BRITTEN (1913-76) AND PETER PEARS (born 1910)
By Kenneth Green, 1943

An early portrait of perhaps the most significant partnership in the history of music. The young composer had met Peter Pears nine years earlier and had already written for him the *Seven Sonnets of Michelangelo* (1940). Their creative partnership found its maturity in the well-known *Serenade for Tenor, Horn and Strings*, written in the same year as the portrait, and Britten continued to write a stream of works for the singer until his death. The painter, Kenneth Green, designed the sets and costumes for the first production of Britten's best-known opera, *Peter Grimes*, performed at Sadler's Wells in 1945 with Pears in the title role.

305 RALPH VAUGHAN WILLIAMS 1872-1958
By Sir Gerald Kelly, 1958-61

This gently realistic but monumental portrait of the composer shows him as 'the grand old man of British music', as he was shortly before his death. It was worked up from studies made in connection with a portrait commissioned for the Royal College of Music in 1953. Vaughan Williams was one of the leading composers of the English musical renaissance in the twentieth century and an important figure in the English folk music revival. His symphonies and choral works are still much played and respected and their stature has, if anything, increased over the years.